D0914342

AMERICAN BAR
ASSOCIATION

PUBLICATION MADE POSSIBLE BY:

ALL AMERICA BANK
BANCFIRST
MR. & MRS. GLENN A. COX
CROWE & DUNLEVY
NADINE HOLLOWAY
THE KERR FOUNDATION, INC.
TOM & PHYLLIS MCCASLAND

OGE ENERGY CORP.
HOMER & RAMONA PAUL
MR. & MRS. C. J. SILAS
JAMES & BARBARA STURDIVANT
WACHTELL, LIPTON, ROSEN & KATZ
HARRY A. WOODS., JR.
   & CAROL M. WOODS

Donna & Walter Allison
Mr. & Mrs. Burck Bailey
Judge & Mrs. Thomas R. Brett
Mr. & Mrs. B. C. Clark, Jr.
Jerry Durbin
Dr. & Mrs. Robert S. Ellis
Ed & Barbara Eskridge
Mr. & Mrs. Allen D. Evans
Mr. & Mrs. John Gaberino, Jr.
Mr. & Mrs. John J. Griffin, Jr.
J. Wenonah Paul Gunning
Mr. & Mrs. James H. Holloman, Jr.
Mr. & Mrs. E. Deane Kanaly

Brooke & Mike Murphy
C. D. Northcutt
David & Sharon Petty
Shirley & DeVier Pierson
Barbara & Charles Renfrew
Dr. & Mrs. Galen Robbins
Mr. & Mrs. J. Hugh Roff, Jr.
Barbara Smith
Bob & Sandy Stein
Don R. & Mary Louise Symcox
Barbara & Blake Tartt
Richard D. & Rae I. Winzeler

11/17/10

To Peggy Weiner:

I'm so glad you agreed to accept this book. You are, after all, only one generation removed from being a Pauls Valley girl. Your father was a great man. Many will miss him. You have a wonderful family and are dear friends.

Willie Paul

WILLIE
of the VALLEY

THE LIFE OF BILL PAUL

By

Bob Burke
and
Eric Dabney

Foreword by
Judge Ralph Thompson

OKLAHOMA TRACKMAKER SERIES

SERIES EDITOR: GINI MOORE CAMPBELL

Printed in the United States of America by Bart Baker Group, LLC & Jostens, Inc. - 405.503.3207

ISBN 978-1-885596-64-2

Library of Congress Catalog Number 2007942044

Designed by Kris Vculek • Cover Photo by John Douglas

OKLAHOMA HERITAGE ASSOCIATION

CONTENTS

Many people helped make this biography possible. Bill's wife, Barbara, spent dozens of hours looking through scrapbooks and boxes of photographs and recalling poignant stories of their life together. Bill sat with a tape recorder and chronicled the most intricate details of his interesting and fulfilled life. His assistants, Joyce Coleson, Pam Gilley, and Janelle Cox, put those words into an organized and readable form. Many of Bill's family and friends, including his children, helped gather information and photographs.

For the early Paul family history, we were assisted by Richard Green, historian of the Chickasaw Nation, Adrienne Grimmett, who has become the historian of Pauls Valley, and Bill's "Aunt Jim," Winona James Gunning, a virtual powerhouse of knowledge of family truths and legends.

Thanks to our editor, Gini Moore Campbell, our proofreaders—Oklahoma Supreme Court Justice Steven W. Taylor and George and Marcia Davis—and Linda Lynn, Melissa Hayer, Mary Phillips, Robin Davison, and Billie Harry at the Oklahoma Publishing Company archives for help in selecting photographs.

We salute the Oklahoma Heritage Association, its president, Shannon Nance, and chairman of the board Glen Johnson, Jr., for its efforts to preserve Oklahoma's colorful and exciting history.

—Bob Burke   *—Eric Dabney*   2007

Attributed to the Founding Fathers, possibly Thomas Jefferson, is this memorable quotation: "Let us dream of an aristocracy of achievement arising out of a democracy of opportunity."

Given their dream, the Founders would have loved William G. Paul. Readers of this fascinating life story of intelligence, ambition, effort, leadership, determination, patriotism, and achievement will surely agree that his has been a life of fulfillment of just such a dream.

Success came early. Leaving the family dairy farm in Pauls Valley, Oklahoma, as his high school's valedictorian, Bill Paul entered the University of Oklahoma, making the highest score on its entrance examination in the University's history. He became the University's Outstanding Male Freshman Student, a member of Phi Beta Kappa, and the Outstanding Male Graduate. As a Marine officer he served in Korea and, eventually, retired as a Marine colonel. At the University of Oklahoma College of Law he graduated with the law's highest recognition of scholarship and a distinguished career as a lawyer began, excelling as a trial lawyer, managing partner of his firm, and as general counsel of Oklahoma's largest corporation.

His ascendancy in leadership included his election as president of the Oklahoma Bar Association, president of the National Conference of Bar Presidents and, ultimately, president of the American Bar Association. As the leader of 404,000 lawyers, the largest voluntary professional organization in the world, he became one of the law's principal international leaders. In that role he has been recognized as a dynamic and respected proponent of democracy, human rights, and the rule of law. During events which included being honored by Queen Elizabeth II, the Prime Minister, and leaders of the bar of Britain, he presided at the rededication of the Magna Carta at Runnymede, unveiling a monument bearing an enduring inscription that he authored – a lasting tribute to the rule of law by one who has dedicated his own life to the rule of law. Admirably, despite his extraordinary successes, he has never forgotten his own modest beginnings and has been committed to helping others. His initiatives and personal philanthropies have promoted diversity and opportunities for minorities in the study of law both nationally and throughout the world.

From a Garvin County farm boy to a world leader of law, this fine man of achievement, undisputably one of America's premier lawyers, is a most deserving and worthy product of the Founders' dream of "democracy of opportunity." This story of his life's journey, so skillfully and movingly told here, will be an inspiration to others who yearn to live the same American dream.

　　　　　—Ralph G. Thompson
　　　　　　Senior United States District Judge

PIONEER HERITAGE

The whites will not allow us to keep our sovereignty. But I dearly hope the memory of the proud Chickasaws will not be forgotten.
— Smith Paul

William George Paul is a member of one of Oklahoma's most colorful pioneer families. Known as "Bill" or "Willie," he was born November 25, 1930, on Paul Avenue in Pauls Valley, Oklahoma. What could be perceived as an aristocratic beginning was anything but—he was born at home in a rented, garage apartment.

The story of the Paul family is full of adventure, violence, achievement, and tragedy. Bill is half-Irish, but his Chickasaw ancestry has largely shaped his life. His 1/16th Chickasaw blood is derived from his great-great grandmother, Ala-Teecha, a Chickasaw full blood who came to Indian Territory in 1837. Ala-Teecha—her English name was Ellen—brought with her stories of the proud and long tradition of the Chickasaw people.

The origin of the Chickasaws is unknown. Some historians speculate the Chickasaws lived before 1300 A.D. west of the Mississippi River, possibly in the Red River Valley. When Europeans encountered them in 1700, the Chickasaws were living in villages in present-day Mississippi, western Tennessee, and South Carolina. They had a reputation for being brave and fierce warriors and were known as the "Unconquered and Unconquerable Chickasaw Nation." The Chickasaws were second only to the Choctaws in Native American population in Mississippi. Prior to 1729, the Natchez also was a large tribe.[1]

After the passage of the Indian Removal Act in 1830, the Chickasaw Nation ceded its lands east of the Mississippi River to the federal government and agreed to relocate in Indian Territory. Of the Five Civilized Tribes, the Chickasaws were among the last to relocate. They first lived on land leased from the Choctaws. In 1855, the Chickasaws separated and relocated to their own territory in southcentral Oklahoma. The following year, the Chickasaws drafted and adopted their own constitution and elected the leadership of a three-branch government.[2]

The Chickasaw Nation was bordered on the north by the South Canadian River and on the south by the Red River. The modern towns of Pauls Valley, Ada, Ardmore, Purcell, Sulphur, Tishomingo, Duncan, Chickasha, Marietta, and Madill are in the Chickasaw Nation.

Bill Paul's great-great grandfather was Smith Paul, a bearded man of Scottish descent. The elder Paul was born in New Bern, North Carolina, on May 27, 1809, the same year Abraham Lincoln was born. Smith's grandfather, Jacob Paul, fought in the Revolutionary War. Smith's mother, Tamsey Paul, died when he was young. When his father, Rhesa Paul, remarried, Smith did not get along well with his stepmother and ran away from home at age 16.

Smith Paul is the name sake of Pauls Valley and patriarch of the Paul family in Oklahoma. *Courtesy Bill and Barbara Paul.*

Ala-Teecha "Ellen" Paul was the wife of Smith Paul. Ellen was a well-educated full-blood Chickasaw. *Courtesy Bill and Barbara Paul.*

Smith wandered around Florida and the Deep South and accompanied two wagon trains headed to California until he was taken in by a Scottish missionary, A.G. McClure, who lived among the Chickasaws in northern Mississippi. McClure's wife, Ala-Teecha, was a full-blood Chickasaw. She was well educated and her sisters married prominent Choctaw leaders such as Peter Maytubby and Solomon Goforth.[3]

In the early 1830s, after it was decided that the Chickasaws would be removed to Oklahoma, Smith volunteered to join a scouting party to Indian Territory led by United States Army officers. The purpose of the trip was to get an advance look at the land that would be the Chickasaws' new home. On the adventurous year-long mission, Smith saw for the first time the fertile valley along the Washita River in southcentral Oklahoma that someday would bear his name.[4]

Smith returned to Mississippi as the Chickasaws began preparations for their trip westward. He rejoined the McClure family and made the difficult journey by land and by steamboat to the Choctaw lands in southeastern Oklahoma in 1837. They settled near Boggy Depot in present day Bryan County.[5]

Soon after arriving in Indian Territory, McClure died, leaving his widow, Ala-Teecha, and two children, Catherine and Tecumseh. Smith stayed with the family and tilled the land to grow corn and vegetables to feed his adopted family. In the early 1840s, Smith married Ala-Teecha. In 1845, Sam Paul, Bill's great grandfather, was born. Smith and Ala-Teecha had two other children, Jesse Paul, who died as a young adult, and a daughter, Sippie Paul. When Sam Paul was less than two years old, the family moved to present-day Garvin County. Soon the area was known as Smith Paul's Valley.[6]

Smith found the rich bottomland along the Washita River to be excellent for farming. Bluestem grass grew so high that a man on horseback was almost hidden in its foliage. Smith was unique in his farming. He grew corn when most other farmers raised cattle. He also was a true pioneer, moving into an area that was a traditional hunting ground for less than friendly Native Americans such as the Comanches and Kiowas.[7]

Smith lived peacefully among the nomadic Plains Indians who frequented the area because he heeded the advice of his Native American wife. Ala-Teecha said, "Never show fear when you see the horse-riding Indians approaching. Don't make any sign or motion that you are afraid of them. Don't close your windows and lock them. Go out and hold out your hand." Ala-Teecha told her husband that Indian visitors should be offered food. She said she had never seen horse-riding Indians who were not hungry and "they were in a better frame of mind after eating." [8]

In 1851, four years after Smith arrived at his new home near the Washita River, he and the few other residents of the area were provided protection by the establishment of Fort Arbuckle nine miles west of present Davis, Oklahoma. Soldiers from the fort, named for Brigadier General Matthew Arbuckle, kept the peace by regularly patrolling nearby settlements and forcing Plains Indian hunting parties away from the area. Fort Arbuckle was garrisoned with federal troops until it was abandoned and taken over by Confederate forces in the Civil War.

Smith was able to choose prime farmland for his own use partly because his wife had full rights as a full-blood Chickasaw. There was no individual ownership of land in the Chickasaw Nation. Chickasaws did not believe it was morally right to own, barter, or trade anything that God had given them to sustain life.

Smith Paul's first home in Pauls Valley was a double-log house on what is now South Walnut Street. He later moved to land on Jackson Hill and last lived in a stone house atop a hill in the city which bears his name. By local standards, Smith became wealthy.

Paul's Valley did not become a city overnight. After the Civil War, other white settlers began to move into the area. The settlement was a stop on the Butterfield Stage that carried mail on a route from Boggy Depot to Fort Sill, Oklahoma. At a two-story log building called Stage Stop, drivers would change their teams, eat supper, stay over night, and head out the next morning for places such as Whitebead Hill, Erin Springs, Rush Springs, and Fort Sill.[9]

In 1868, Smith became aware that some of his Caddo Indian neighbors in Cherokee Town, north of present Wynnewood, were being decimated by smallpox. Indians were overcrowded, poorly housed, and had little food or medical supplies.[10]

When Smith asked the War Department for help, he was appointed an agent to the Caddo. Smith took matters into his own hands and moved the sick Indians closer to his home in Pauls Valley. Unfortunately, smallpox took not only the lives of many of the Caddoes, but Smith's eight-month-old grandson, Hogan, died from the disease. His grave was the first marked in the old cemetery at Pauls Valley.[11]

Paul's Valley had its first post office beginning in 1871. It was established in the home of T.F. Waite, halfway between Paul's Valley and Cherokee Town. Waite's home became the oldest post office in continuous existence in the Chickasaw Nation.[12]

Paul's Valley began to grow as a community with the arrival of the Santa Fe Railroad in 1887. The railroad was expanding in southern Oklahoma and officials decided that Smith Paul's Valley should be a principal stop along its north-south route through Indian Territory. However, the railroad dropped the name Smith because the railroad sign painter thought the entire town's name was too long to paint on each end of the depot. The signs simply said, "Paul's Valley." The apostrophe remained in the town's name until shortly after 1900.[13]

Along the well-worn trail from Boggy Depot to Fort Sill also traveled long wagon trains of supplies to feed the soldiers at Fort Sill and large bands of Comanche and Kiowa Indians that had been rounded up by federal troops. Often, Comanches accompanied troops on missions to retrieve supplies from Boggy Depot. In a 1984 newspaper interview, Bill's uncle, Haskell Paul, chronicled a Comanche visit to Pauls Valley:

> *Both men and horses arrived coated with dust and sweat. The soldiers took the Comanches from downtown about where it is now—to the current location of Lee Middle School. They would buy the Indians live beef animals and supply them with bread. The Comanches would slaughter the cattle and prepare their meals on the spot.*[14]

As more settlers arrived in Pauls Valley, churches, stores, and other commercial structures were built. Church bells tolled when a resident died. J.M. Hazlitt, in his short history of Pauls Valley, talked about other sounds that characterized the town:

There was the whooping of horsemen who gave vent
to loud yells when riding into or out of town at a dead
run. There was the clump of horses hooves on the
parched streets or the slop, slop, slop when mud took
over…There were the shouts of wagon drivers and
the rumble and clatter of all sizes and shapes of wagons.
There were the "giddaps" and "whoa's" and other
language, much unprintable, that went with horses,
mules and oxen.[15]

Smith's wife, Ala-Teecha, died in 1871 and Smith
married a local schoolteacher, Sarah Ann "Annie" Lilley, a
short time later.

Smith prospered greatly in his farming and ranching
operation. He supported businesses that sprang up because
of settlers moving into his valley. Ambrose Klinglesmith,
who wore his hair in braids, operated a blacksmith shop. C.J.
Grant and Thomas Martin opened a general store.

The Chickasaw Nation saw much more change than
just in agriculture. The increase of white settlers resulted in
the formation of two political parties in the bitterly-divided
Chickasaw Nation. A Progressive Party favored integration
with and assimilation into the culture of the white settlers.
The Conservative Party, on the other hand, espoused a more
isolationist view and attempted to exclude whites from
positions of power in the Chickasaw Nation.[16]

Smith Paul's son, Sam, became a leader in the
Progressive Party and served in the Chickasaw Senate. He
started the *Pauls Valley Enterprise* and later bought a press
and established a newspaper in Ardmore. He was a colorful,
passionate, violent, and charismatic man. For a time he was

An old postcard shows Smith Paul's home in Pauls Valley. *Courtesy Bill and Barbara Paul.*

a Chickasaw law officer, a job in which he was forced to kill suspected horse thieves and other criminals. However, Sam did not always need a legal reason to kill someone.

Bill Paul III and his wife, Cindy Paul, in their book, *Shadow of an Indian Star*, trace Sam's dark history. Even though the book is admittedly historical fiction, it is based upon substantial research into the lives of the Paul family, including a review of Sam's many brushes with the law.[17]

More than once Sam was charged with murder. On one occasion he was tried before the legendary federal judge, Isaac Parker, "the hanging judge," in Fort Smith, Arkansas.[18] Sam was acquitted in all his trials except the last one. He was convicted of manslaughter and sentenced to ten years in a federal prison. When his supporters in the Chickasaw Nation

Sam Paul was a leader in the Chickasaw Nation. He and his great-grandson, Bill Paul, are both members of the Chickasaw Hall of Fame. Bill was inducted in 2002, and Sam was posthumously inducted in 2004. *Courtesy Bill and Barbara Paul.*

came to his aid, he was granted a pardon by President Grover Cleveland.

Chickasaw politics may have resulted in Sam's death on December 19, 1891. He was shot to death by his son, Joe. Sam was only 46 years old. Legend has it that his political enemies convinced Joe to kill his father, although rumors circulated that a long family dispute resulted in the tragic family killing.   Later, Joe was assassinated and family stories attribute his demise to his half-brother, William H. Paul. If true, it was "an eye-for-an-eye," retribution for Joe killing their father. Joe's cousin was arrested for his murder, but was acquitted.[19]

Sam's death was big news in the Chickasaw Nation. Every newspaper ran front-page stories and called the murder "expected." The Indian Journal said, "As erred the sire, so erred the son." *The Chickasaw Chieftain* wrote, "It was a brutal murder; a most heinous crime. Yet it was but the anticipated tragic ending of a feud between father and son." [20]

Even though it was expected, Sam's death was a tragedy for the Chickasaw Nation that was deprived of his leadership in such a critical time of transition from Indian sovereignty to statehood. Just two months before his death, Sam had been quoted in an issue of *The Chickasaw Chieftain*, his newspaper printed at Ardmore, Oklahoma. The quotes became known as Sam Paul's Prophecy of Oklahoma statehood:

"*I said before this progress is carrying us toward Statehood... The beginning of the end is here. The State of Oklahoma, if such it will be called, will include the old bounds of the Indian Territory. No State west of the Mississippi River will surpass it in the extent and variety of its resources and general prosperity of its people…Men of Indian blood will sit beside their white brethren in the councils of state and assist in the administration of government. Their interest will be mutual. Their races will be blended as one. The Indian problem will no longer cry for solution. Civilization will have broken down the last barrier raised to retard her irresistible march. Our hills and valleys will teem with industry and thrift and our streams turn the wheels of manufactories. Important trade centers and roadways of commerce will spring up along the old cattle trails and stage roads. One of the grandest commonwealths in American union will be built here. I have given you no fancy sketch. The time is not far off.*" [21]

Sam's prophetic words were uncannily true. Oklahoma would become the 46th state just 16 years later.

The fabric of the Chickasaws' ancient culture was further tested when the federal government questioned the tradition of holding land in common. Much of the push for individual ownership came from Kansas United States Senator Charles Curtis, later vice president of the United States. The Atoka Agreement of 1897 eventually gave Native American enrollees individual plots of land and the Dawes Commission

The gravestone that marks the place of Smith Paul's burial in Pauls Valley. *Courtesy Bill and Barbara Paul.*

began a political and legal process of winding up the affairs of the Five Civilized Tribes and incorporating them into the new State of Oklahoma. Unfortunately, with the sweeping changes in Chickasaw society and government, the Paul family fortune began to erode.

Two years after Sam was killed, his father, Smith Paul, died on August 18, 1893. On his death bed, legend has it that Smith wrote a note to his stepson, Tecumseh McClure, also a senator in the Chickasaw Nation. The note, probably fictional, but nonetheless with a ring of truth to it, read in part:

> "*I sometimes wonder how things might have turned out had we stood our ground in Mississippi. Then, too, I wonder how things might have come to pass had Sam lived. But all such thinking is folly, for Mississippi is but a dream…Now it is time for both myself and the [Chickasaw] Nation to pass into history. The whites will not allow our people to keep their sovereignty. But I dearly hope that the memory of these proud people will not be forgotten.*" [22]

Smith was buried in the old cemetery at Pauls Valley. His spacious gravesite is marked with an appropriate inscription, "He was the first to make this valley yield of its wealth."

LIFE ON THE FARM

Living on the farm taught us the value of hard work,
but convinced us that we did not want to bale hay and
milk cows for the rest of our lives.
—Homer Paul, Jr.

William Hiram "W.H." Paul, Bill's grandfather, was born
in Smith Paul's Valley on March 5, 1876. He had to grow up
quickly with the loss of his father at age 15. He soon fell in
love with Victoria May Rosser of nearby Wynnewood. She
had arrived in Indian Territory by wagon when she was 11
years old.

Victoria's father, J.T. Rosser, served under General
Robert E. Lee as a captain in the Confederate Army. After
the Civil War he settled on a plantation in Calhoun County,
Mississippi, where Victoria was born on March 31, 1877. In
1889, Rosser decided to take his family westward. He drove
wagons pulled by horses and oxen from Mississippi into
Indian Territory.

The family stopped at the tiny settlement of Muskogee
but wanted to push farther into the wide open spaces of

the new frontier. Rosser heard about rich farmland along
the Washita River in southcentral Oklahoma. He loaded
his wagons and began what turned out to be a trip of
several months over rough country. When he saw Smith
Paul's Valley, he knew he had found his family's land of
opportunity.[1]

Rosser traded his ox team, a tent, and a few horses to
John Burks for a lease on land near the town of Paul's Valley
that contained a two-room log house. Rosser and his oldest
son began putting the prairie land into cultivation. In need of
a school, Rosser and his neighbors bought a frame building in
Paul's Valley and moved it near his home six miles southwest
of town. They called the school Red Branch.[2]

Even before statehood in 1907, Pauls Valley was a
modern town in the Chickasaw portion of Indian Territory.
It had the largest cotton compress in the region, a paid fire
department, an ice plant, an electric light plant, a teachers
association, and was the first city in Indian Territory to
have a free school. Pauls Valley was the hub of a rich and
fertile agricultural area with huge crop yields from the rich
bottomland. The town became known as the "Queen City of
the Washita." [3]

The Rossers joined many other families moving to Pauls
Valley in the last years of the nineteenth century. A newspaper
article claimed that the proximity of the town to the American
desert "assures a constantly recurring supply of pure, dry
air, and is a perfect protection against the hot nights which
prevail in the summer." A reporter in The Valley News wrote,
"Winter is neither long nor severe, being so blended with

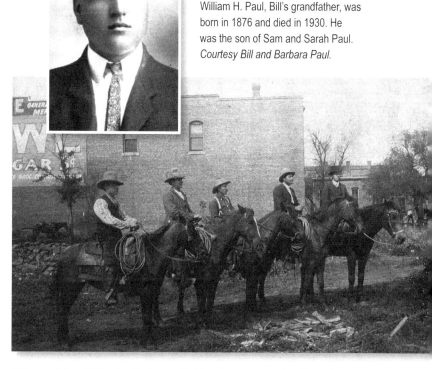

William H. Paul, Bill's grandfather, was born in 1876 and died in 1930. He was the son of Sam and Sarah Paul. *Courtesy Bill and Barbara Paul.*

Bill's grandfather, William H. Paul, competed in rodeos as a member of a roping team. At left is Jesse Chisholm, for whom the Chisholm Trail is named. Paul is second from right. *Courtesy Bill and Barbara Paul.*

a prolonged autumn and an early spring that its identity is almost lost, save for an occasional gust of icy wind and flurry of snow."

Before his marriage to Victoria Rosser, W.H. was sent off to school at Hargrove College in Ardmore, Savoy College at Savoy, Texas, and Austin College in Sherman, Texas. W.H.

Victoria Paul, Bill's grandmother, shown later in life at the 1954 dedication of the Pauls Valley Cemetery. *Courtesy Bill and Barbara Paul.*

and Victoria were married on November 30, 1898. They had ten children, but two of them died in early childhood. The oldest son, William George Paul, nicknamed "Willie," was killed in a tragic family accident in 1927. Three years later when Bill was born, he inherited his uncle's nickname.

Willie's death was a closely-guarded family secret. In fact, Bill never heard the story until he was a teenager and an old family friend told him about it. W.H. had a long-standing problem with alcohol, had lost his business, and was employed as a night watchman. In that job, he carried a gun. When he walked outside his home to shoot a stray dog, his son, Willie, wrapped his arms around the animal. W.H. shot at the dog, but the bullet struck Willie in the chest. He died 30 minutes later.[5]

W.H. and Victoria's second son was Bill's father, Homer Paul, named for Homer's *Odyssey*, born on August 4, 1904. W.H. died from the lingering effects of alcoholism on September 22, 1930. He left his family a home, but very little money. *The Pauls Valley Enterprise* said W.H., "in his days of bodily strength," had served on the city council, was a 32nd-degree Mason, and a member of the Presbyterian church.[6]

Because his father was sick much of the time, Homer had effectively become the head of the household at age 23 when his older brother Willie was killed. Homer's passion was public service. While yet in high school he became interested

The W.H. and Victoria Paul home on Pine Street in Pauls Valley. Bill and his brother, Homer, Jr., spent a lot of time with their grandmother. *Courtesy Bill and Barbara Paul.*

Homer Paul, Bill's father, was a respected member of the Oklahoma legislature. In 2007, Bill and his brother, Homer, Jr., created the Senator Homer Paul Memorial Scholarship for Pauls Valley High School. *Courtesy Bill and Barbara Paul.*

Helen Lafferty Paul, Bill's mother, was born in Indian Territory just three months before Oklahoma statehood in 1907. *Courtesy Bill and Barbara Paul.*

in government and politics. He was elected at age 21 to the Oklahoma House of Representatives in 1926, serving Garvin County in the Eleventh Oklahoma legislature. He was admitted to the bar in 1938. When not in Oklahoma City serving his constituents, Homer had a general practice of law in Pauls Valley.

Homer served three two-year terms in the House of Representatives before being elected to the Oklahoma State Senate in 1932 where he served four, four-year terms, representing citizens of Garvin, McClain, and Cleveland counties. In the Senate, Homer was elected to the third highest position in state government, President Pro Tempore.[7]

After Homer served one term in the legislature, he married Helen Verna Lafferty, born in Foyil, Indian Territory, on August 13, 1907, just three months before Oklahoma statehood. Helen was the daughter of a Methodist preacher who lived at the time in Claremore. Growing up, one of Helen's favorite memories was when Oklahoma humorist Will Rogers rubbed his hands through her blonde hair while visiting with her parents.[8]

Homer and Helen were married in Oklahoma City in the home of his longtime friend, James C. Nance of Purcell. Homer and Nance were serving together in the House of Representatives at the time and both were becoming forces in Oklahoma politics. In the 1929 legislative session, they joined a handful of other Democrats and most Republicans in impeaching Governor Henry Johnston and putting the very popular lieutenant governor, William J. Holloway, into the governor's mansion for the remaining two years of Johnston's term.[9]

Holloway was among the first of Homer's friends to take note how well he had done by convincing Helen to marry him. Once when Holloway was presiding over the State Senate, he noticed Helen sitting next to Homer in the gallery. Holloway later remarked, "Who was that beautiful blonde sitting next to you?" [10]

Homer and Helen rented a garage apartment on Paul Avenue in Pauls Valley. There, Bill was born on November 25, 1930. When Bill was two years old, the family moved to a farm about two miles southwest of Pauls Valley. The original farm contained approximately 200 acres but was later expanded to 340 acres. Soon after moving to the farm, a second son, Homer Paul, Jr., was born.

Homer had a house built in a less than desirable location on the property because the building site was part of the only 10 acres not mortgaged to the bank. Later, when the mortgage was paid, Homer had the house moved to a location overlooking the valley.[11]

Life on the farm was difficult, but normal for rural Oklahoma in the 1930s. The state had been gripped by the Great Depression, the worst economic downturn and period of high unemployment in modern history. The Depression had begun with the stock market crash in 1929, the year before Bill's birth, and worsened as banks failed, stores and factories closed, and millions of Americans were left jobless and homeless.

Oklahoma and Garvin County suffered greatly during the Great Depression. The economy was based largely on agriculture which was devastated by falling market prices. In addition to the economic problems, a searing drought hit the southern plains until even normally wet Garvin County was scorched. To the west, the state was wracked with dust storms. Sand blew so thickly that travelers lost their way, chickens went to roost at noon, airports closed, and trains stopped. Animals and humans suffered from the blowing dust.[12]

Much of Homer's time was spent studying legislative proposals to lessen the effect of the Great Depression upon Oklahoma. Homer backed efforts by Governors Holloway and William H. "Alfalfa Bill" Murray to make jobs by appropriating state dollars to upgrade Oklahoma's highway system. Oklahoma became the first state to appropriate money for the needy.[13]

Homer served in a tumultuous time in the political history of Oklahoma. He saw one governor, Johnston, thrown out of office and another governor make national headlines by his bold use of the National Guard to carry out his edicts. Governor Murray activated the National Guard 34 times during his administration from 1931 to 1934. He made the cover of *Time Magazine* after using the National Guard to defy a federal judge's order to make a bridge across the Red River a toll bridge.[14]

One of Homer's greatest challenges in the State Senate was to carefully consider proposals of Governor Murray and his successor, Ernest W. Marland, the founder of the oil company that became Conoco. Especially troubling was Governor Marland's efforts to use much of the state budget to match federal funds appropriated as part of President Franklin Roosevelt's New Deal program to spur the nation's recovery from the Depression.[15]

Homer supported federal construction projects in his district. He recognized that his unemployed constituents and the community would benefit from the construction of buildings and parks by the Works Projects Administration (WPA) and the National Youth Administration (NYA). Homer praised such programs at the dedication of a new NYA building in Pauls Valley in May, 1938. The town was so proud of its new building that Mayor Mason Hart proclaimed a two-hour holiday so town workers could attend the dedication and "partake of the giant barbecue feast." [16]

Homer was part of a group of strong rural legislators who

wanted rural development, tax relief, subsistence homesteads, and more state assistance for farmers and ranchers who were devastated by the effects of the long-term drought and plummeting of commodity prices.[17]

Until Bill was six years old, the Paul farm home did not have electricity or natural gas. His mother cooked on a wood stove and the house was heated by a wood-burning fireplace. A windmill pumped water into an elevated storage tank and provided running water to the kitchen. There was no indoor bathroom so the family used an outhouse located in a prominent position from the back door.[18]

The Paul family bathed in a large washtub placed on the kitchen floor. Helen poured water heated on the wood stove into the tub. Food was kept cold in an icebox, a wooden structure that contained 50-pound blocks of ice purchased in town. A radio ran on battery power, supplemented by a small wind-powered generator attached to the roof of the house.[19]

In 1936, the quality of life was greatly improved when electricity and natural gas came to the area. A modern bathroom was added to the house, a hot water tank was installed, Helen began cooking on a gas range, and a natural gas furnace provided heat. An electric pump was placed in the hand-dug water well. For the first time, hot and cold running water was piped to the kitchen and bathroom.[20]

Bill's father was an astute politician who daily read newspapers and kept up with what was happening in the state and nation. He was a strong supporter of Congressman Lyle H. Boren, the father of Governor, United States Senator, and University of Oklahoma President David L. Boren. Homer applauded Boren during the Depression after Boren blasted author John Steinbeck's portrayal of "Okies" in his book, *The Grapes of Wrath*. Boren called Steinbeck's novel a "dirty, lying, filthy manuscript," and said the book exposed nothing but "the total depravity, vulgarity, and degraded mentality of the author." Boren told Congress, "The grapes of wrath that Steinbeck would father in a world of truth and right would press for him the bitter drink of just condemnation and isolation for his unclean mind." [21]

In 1937, Bill's father threw his hat into the ring with 20 other candidates for the Fifth District congressional post. In the Democratic primary, Homer ran second to the eventual winner, Gomer Smith. Among the Democratic contenders who ran behind Homer in popularity at the polls were later United States Senator Mike Monroney, legendary lawyer Moman Pruiett, and Congressman F.B. Swank.

Homer attributed his fine showing in the congressional race to the fact that three of the seven counties that made up the congressional district were counties he represented in the State Senate. Homer was not required to give up his State Senate seat because he was in the middle of a four-year term.[22]

Bill began his formal education at Lee Elementary School. The people of Pauls Valley had a proud history of supporting public schools. At statehood the school district was considered among the best in Oklahoma. *Sturm's Oklahoma Magazine* wrote in 1907, "The public school system in Pauls Valley is equal to any town in either territory, and is superior to most towns of its size in the older, settled states." [23]

Because Homer was in the legislature that met only once

every two years, he moved his family to Oklahoma City to an apartment during the first half of the year for the legislative session. As a result, Bill attended the second semester of his first grade year at Lincoln School in northeast Oklahoma City. He later attended Edgemere School in the Crown Heights section of the capital city for the second semester of his third and fifth years in elementary school.[24]

Bill, standing, and his brother, Homer, Jr., in 1938. They spent their daylight hours working on the farm and playing with friends. Courtesy Bill and Barbara Paul.

The Paul farmhouse on top of a hill near Pauls Valley. *Courtesy Bill and Barbara Paul.*

Their aunt, Winona James "Aunt Jim" Gunning, remembered Bill as a smart, well-liked, patient, student who was "amazingly inquisitive." Bill was sober and serious and a very active leader.[25]

Homer was a firm believer in giving his two sons plenty of work. He was busy being a senator and lawyer and did not have time to be a full-time farmer. He assigned much of the farm work to Bill and Homer, Jr. The boys oversaw the planting, cultivation, and harvesting of their primary cash crop, alfalfa. They also planted corn, wheat, and oats to feed their growing dairy cattle herd.

They peddled excess milk to families in Pauls Valley in quart jars. Homer, Jr., remembered, "We milked early in the morning and late in the afternoon. We had Jerseys that gave high butterfat, some Guernseys. Later we bought Holsteins. We could tell how rich the milk was by how far the cream line came down the jar." [26]

Much of the day-to-day farming instruction came from Bill's mother who grew up on a farm. Helen knew how to milk cows and grow gardens. She was a striking woman, five feet seven inches tall, blonde, and beautiful. She was serious and conscientious about the Methodist church and raised her sons in that tradition. They were in Sunday School each week and attended church camp in the summer. Bill said, "She was a great foundation for the family. Whenever my brother and I needed her, she was there for us and helped guide us through the various crises of our lives." [27]

Homer, Jr. described his mother as "versatile with a strong personality." He said, "She could be comfortable

The dairy barn where Bill and his brother, Homer, Jr., spent many hours caring for the cattle and producing milk for delivery to neighbors. *Courtesy Homer Paul.*

Bill riding his favorite horse, Lady Bob, in 1941. Bill's parents believed that their boys should have plenty of time to enjoy life on the farm. *Courtesy Bill and Barbara Paul.*

working on the farm, milking cows, doing chores, or visiting the governor's mansion." While their father was volatile, Helen was steady, a dynamic that served Bill and Homer, Jr. well into their formative years.[28]

Homer had an entrepreneurial streak in him and perhaps would have done well in business had politics not been the principal focus of his life. On one occasion, he bought a herd of Jacks and Jennetts in partnership with Tom Berry of

Stillwater. People drove from miles around to see the unusual long-eared animals that grazed on the Paul farm. The venture was commercially successful because of the great value of Jacks used to breed mares to produce mules to be sold as work animals. Mules cannot reproduce, so reproduction had to be accomplished by the use of Jacks and mares.[29]

Other interesting ranching experiments Homer undertook included the purchase of several Percheron mares, huge draft horses used to work the farm and for use as brood mares for mule colts. For a time, the Pauls raised mixed-blood Arabian horses and registered Hereford cattle. They sold young bulls to area cattlemen for breeding stock.[30]

Homer loved animals. A small flock of bantam chickens were used to set quail eggs. Bill remembered, "Those little hens tried so hard to be good mothers to the 20 or so quail they would hatch, but the hens couldn't run as fast as the baby quail—it was a hard life for the hens." The boys also had a pet raccoon, a pet deer, and at least one bird dog.[31]

When Bill was six and Homer, Jr., four, their father gave them a coal-black Shetland pony they named "Queen." The boys shared both a bedroom and their horses. Queen was bred and produced a paint colt they named "Prince." It was quite a sight to see the small ponies mingle with the huge Percheron mares in the pasture. When the larger horses sniffed Prince, Queen laid her ears back, ran toward the mares, and kicked both hind legs as if she had no understanding of the size difference and her obvious disadvantage in any confrontation. Oddly enough, the bluff worked. The Percheron mares would turn tail and trot away.[32]

The day of the mule and large draft horses faded into history with the advent of tractors that became affordable for those on family farms. In 1938, Homer acquired a Farmall F-20 and the basic implements to go with it. Bill and Homer, Jr. learned to drive the tractor on which they would spend a good portion of their lives.

As with most brothers, Bill and Homer, Jr., often fought. Because Bill was two years older, he won most of the early skirmishes. However, Homer, Jr. was more athletic than Bill and rapidly caught up to Bill's prowess as a fighter. One day while mowing on the tractor in the pasture, the sickle bar became clogged for what seemed like the 40th time of the day. Bill asked Homer, Jr. to clear the bar. Homer, Jr. refused, saying it was Bill's turn. The brothers agreed to settle the decision with a fight. It was close—Homer, Jr. almost won. That was the last fight the boys had.[33]

Bill feeding the chickens on the Paul farm. Daily chores were part of his everyday routine. *Courtesy Bill and Barbara Paul.*

GROWING INTO A MAN

*With our parents looking over our shoulders, we had no choice but
to be law-abiding and mannerly young men.*

— Bill Paul

Bill was guided in his early years by his father's sense of
public service and his mother's sense of doing what was
right. Bill's Aunt Jim Gunning said, "Helen instilled the love
of Pauls Valley in her boys. She blended seamlessly into the
family when Homer, known by the family as 'Snip,' brought
her home to marry."[1]

"Helen was patient and kind and well-liked," Aunt Jim
remembered, "and Willie received those exact characteristics
from her. Snip was energetic and always talkative and
outgoing. He and Helen made such a good match that Willie
could emulate both of them." [2] Helen was also a fabulous
cook. Her specialties were chicken fried steak with creamed
gravy, fried chicken, and pot roast.[3]

Bill also was influenced by a loving grandmother,
Victoria Paul. Bill and Homer, Jr. spent many nights at their

grandmother's house, climbing into cold beds in the winter
with heated bricks wrapped in towels to warm their feet.
Bill loved to say to Victoria, "Grandmother, tell us about
those territory days." As the boys drifted off to sleep, their
grandmother told of the days when oxen carts pulled her
to town and how she loved to ride side-saddle and spend
afternoons target shooting.[4]

Grandmother Paul was fiercely loyal to her family,
strong, and always interested in the political life of her
community and state. She founded the local Red Cross
chapter and was instrumental in preserving the stories of
Pauls Valley's pioneers. She later led the effort to restore
the Old Cemetery in Pauls Valley where so many of her
family members were buried. She also took up painting. Her
charcoals and oil paintings won prizes at the county fair. And,
she insisted her grandsons be exposed to classic literature and
fine music.[5]

The family farm provided a great training ground for
a good work ethic and a splendid venue for play. There
was always plenty of work caring for cattle and horses and
bringing in crops of alfalfa and small grains. "Growing up
on a farm," Homer, Jr., said, "teaches you responsibility. The
cows don't care if it's your birthday, if it's raining, or if it's
Christmas. They have to be milked twice a day and fed." It
was a healthy, honest lifestyle that by its nature taught Bill
and Homer, Jr. the value of hard work and accomplishment of
assigned tasks.[6]

Fence building was a necessary task on the farm. Once
when Homer and his sons broke for lunch in the middle
of a day-long fencing project, Homer received a call that

the governor and lieutenant governor were both out of state, making him, as Senate President Pro Tempore, the acting governor. The caller asked if Homer was interested in traveling to Oklahoma City to spend the day "being the governor." Homer replied, " No, I'm building fence with my boys." Bill and Homer, Jr. had fun for the rest of day, yelling things such as, "Hey, Governor, come over here with your hammer!" [7]

There was plenty of time for recreation on the Paul farm. Robert D. "Bob" Fields joined Bill and Homer, Jr., fishing and swimming in the pond or playing in the barn made of huge timbers. The structure sat on a hill and could be seen for miles around.[8]

Bill was glad to entertain his own friends and children of his father's friends on the farm. Nadine Norton Holloway remembers days of running through the fields and playing in the spacious top floor of the barn.[9] Lou Lindsey Hall was younger than Bill but often accompanied her older brother to the farm. She said, "Bill was very patient with me and taught me to ride a horse, milk a cow, and drive a tractor." Bill also taught Hall the importance of history by stopping at every roadside historical marker.[10]

School was an important part of Bill's life, whether he was at home in Pauls Valley or, in grade school years, in Oklahoma City during his father's legislative sessions. The adjustment period in split school years was difficult, but Bill and Homer, Jr., made friends and successfully transitioned back and forth from a small school to a large city school.[11]

Even though Bill scored amazing academic successes later in school, he came in second in a spelling bee between the third and fourth grade classes at Lee School. William J. Robinson, now an Oklahoma City attorney, was a year behind Bill and ended up in a spell-off with Bill. Robinson won the contest by spelling "February." Robinson remembered, "That was a rare win against Willie. Thereafter, his meteoric scholarship achievements are the stuff of which legends are made." [12]

The Paul family in 1945. Left to right, Homer, Homer, Jr., Helen, and Bill. *Courtesy Bill and Barbara Paul.*

From the sixth grade through high school, Bill attended Pauls Valley schools exclusively. He was eleven years old and in the sixth grade when the Japanese attacked Pearl Harbor on December 7, 1941, and America entered World War II.

As with other families, the Pauls' way of life was affected. Gasoline and food were rationed. Bill and Homer, Jr. collected scrap metal for use in the war effort and his parents bought war bonds and stamps. No automobiles or farm equipment were manufactured for civilian use. Several family members volunteered for military service including Bill's father who served 18 months in the United States Navy.[13]

Athletic competition helped shape Bill's life. Tradition-rich high school football was the sport of choice in Pauls Valley. In 1935, a decade before Bill tried out for the team, Pauls Valley claimed the Oklahoma-Texas bi-state high school championship, having defeated Central High School of Oklahoma City for the Oklahoma crown, and Breckinridge, Texas, for the bi-state title. Bill went out for the team his sophomore year. His teammate and best friend, Bob Fields, described him as "small and quick." Bill played only in enough games to win a letter that year.[14]

The following year a new coach, Otis Delaporte, an outstanding athlete at Central State College in Edmond, Oklahoma, and a Navy veteran, introduced the Split-T formation. Bill was placed in the right guard position and was a starter on both offense and defense his final two years of high school. Bill's junior season was a rebuilding year but Coach Delaporte put together an excellent team in 1947. An Oklahoma City sportswriter called the team, "the best little 135-pound team in the state." At 160 pounds, Bill was the second heaviest man on the team.[15]

For a small town—Pauls Valley had about 6,000 people at the time—the 1947 football season was a great success, especially if consideration is given to the size of the schools on the schedule. With only 67 in the Pauls Valley senior class, games were played against much larger schools. Pauls Valley won six of nine games, including wins over Ardmore, for the first time in a dozen years, Duncan, Durant, and Crooked Oak High School in Oklahoma City.[16]

Most of the wins were upsets, especially the victory over Crooked Oak, a high-scoring team with a talented halfback, Frank Silva, who later was named All-State and played football at the University of Oklahoma. Pauls Valley shut down Silva that night and won by two touchdowns. Bill and his teammates lost that year to Chickasha, Ada, and Seminole. Sam Allen of Chickasha, Don Summers of Ada, and Tommy Gray of Seminole all went on to play college football.

Bob Fields played left halfback on the high school team. Fields was small but was from a family of athletes. The Fields family was famous for owning and operating Field's Tavern in Pauls Valley, a popular place for townspeople and travelers alike. The tavern is gone but Field's pecan pies still are sold.[17]

The right halfback, Charles Montgomery, was very fast and ran through holes carved out by Bill and other linemen. Montgomery was All-State and five players, including Bill, were named to the All-District team. In the state playoffs, Pauls Valley was eliminated by Hugo in a heartbreaking game played in a rainstorm with about two inches of water on the field. Bill was nearly tossed out of the game for arguing with a referee about a Hugo player crossing the goal line that

Bill, second from left, appears in "Jane Eyre" at Pauls Valley High School in 1947. His good friend, Bob Fields, is on the couch. *Courtesy Bill and Barbara Paul.*

had been washed away by the rain. Bill said, "I could see no evidence that the ball crossed the line—and neither could the referee." [18]

Other members of the Pauls Valley football team included Ray Cotten, Jim Hart, Don Brim, Bob Maxwell, Raymond Chaufty, and Kenneth Morris. Bill believed his experience in high school football taught him a valuable lesson to rejoice in team victory as well as individual victory. High school football was the only team sport Bill seriously played.

Coach Delaporte instilled teamwork in his players. Delaporte, who later coached at Clinton, Oklahoma, High School, Southwestern State College at Weatherford, Oklahoma, and was an assistant coach at Oklahoma State University, knew how to motivate his players. Before

most games he worked up some scheme to get Bill and his
teammates fired up. Once he claimed to have found a letter
written to the opposing coach from the coach of the team
Pauls Valley had played the week before. Delaporte read the
letter that included a reference to Bill, "Anytime you need
three yards, all you have to do is run over No. 23 [Bill's
number]."

Bill took the field determined there would be no three
yards gained through his guard hole. Pauls Valley won the
game. It was not until after the victory that players questioned
the authenticity of the letter.

One Halloween night, Bill was the ringleader in a
clandestine operation to haul an abandoned outhouse and
place it on Coach Delaporte's front lawn. The coach was a
good sport and seemingly enjoyed the attention. He made a
positive out of the prank by using wood from the outhouse to
fuel a bonfire at the school pep rally the following week.

Another of Bill's extracurricular activities was high
school band. He played the slide trombone, although he
almost drove his younger brother crazy playing "Twinkle
Twinkle Little Star" over and over during practice sessions.
Austin Kidwell was a gifted band director who could play
and teach all instruments. Kidwell, whose son, Kent, is a
distinguished music professor at the University of Central
Oklahoma and principal trombone player in the Oklahoma
City Philharmonic Orchestra, was strong on discipline.
His marching bands frequently took honors at the Tri-State
Music Festival on the campus of Phillips University in Enid,
Oklahoma.[19]

Throughout his years in junior high school and Pauls Valley High School, Bill was encouraged by competent and dedicated teachers. He was a serious student and was motivated to achieve academically. Bob Fields remembered, "He was full of energy and highly competitive. He was great in math—he blew everyone away." [20] Bill completed high school in 1948 with straight As and as valedictorian of his class. His high school English teacher, Emma Lou Carleton, became a significant influence in his future.[21]

Mrs. Carleton took a special interest in Bill, directing and guiding him through selective reading of novelists such as Thomas Wolfe, Aldous Huxley, James Joyce, Howard Fast, and Leo Tolstoy. She assisted Bill in taking a dozen aptitude tests which surely improved his score on future tests that brought him academic success. Mrs. Carleton's husband, R.E., was the high school principal and also was a positive influence on Bill's development. Another teacher, Mabel Erwin, gave Bill additional math work and tutoring and improved his prowess in advanced algebra, geometry, and trigonometry.[22]

In Bill's senior year in high school, Mrs. Carleton arranged for him to compete in a national competition sponsored by a major corporation. The prize was a four-year scholarship for high school seniors who were at the top of their class. When the test results were received on the first aptitude test, Bill discovered he was in the top one percent in the nation.[23]

In the end, Bill did not win a scholarship, but Reford Bond of Chickasha, Oklahoma, Bill's good friend later at the

University of Oklahoma (OU), did. Looking back, Bill was glad he did not win the scholarship. If he had succeeded, he may have gone to college outside Oklahoma and would have missed his marvelous experience at OU.

All of Bill's time was not spent milking cows and studying for school. He and his brother were accomplished cowboys because saddle horses always were present on the farm. In the summer before his senior year, Bill noticed a story in the local newspaper about the annual rodeo and a $50 prize for any local boy who could ride a mule known as "One-Jump Annie" for more than one jump. Annie never had been successfully ridden, but the prize money and Bill's self confidence in his riding ability lured him into the challenge.[24]

As the day to ride the mule approached, Bill's mother pleaded with him not to try to ride the animal. Bill had second thoughts. He visualized Annie as a huge animal about eight feet high, weighing about 2,000 pounds, that snorted flames from her nostrils. However, he was committed. The afternoon before the rodeo, Helen ironed Bill a fresh pair of blue jeans, crying intermittently between last-minute pleas to get him to change his mind.[25]

Bill's father was out of town so his mother and brother accompanied him to the rodeo. About midway through the performance, the announcer summoned Bill, the only person to answer the newspaper challenge, to report to the chutes where the mule awaited. When Bill came face to face with Annie, he was astonished. She was a docile animal, about five feet high, and could not have weighed more than a Shetland pony. His confidence returned. He thought, "How can I possibly miss besting this mule?" [26]

Some real cowboys helped Bill climb over the top of the chute and put him astride Annie bareback. He inserted his hand into a rope drawn taut around the belly of the animal. When the announcer yelled, "And here comes Willie Paul out of Chute No. 2 on One-Jump Annie," the gate flew open and Annie exploded. Bill remembered, "It was as if she was suddenly possessed by a demon. I'm still not sure what she did, but it was some form of twisting and contortions that made it impossible to stay on board." Bill went flying into the dust of the arena floor. He survived with no broken bones, no glory, some loss of dignity, but with his pride intact. Annie stood a few feet away, once more her docile self, no doubt looking at Bill and thinking, in her animal way, "Nobody rides Annie!" [27]

At a Rainbow Girls dance in Pauls Valley in 1947 are, left to right, Bob Milnor, Jim Hart, and Bill. *Courtesy Bill and Barbara Paul.*

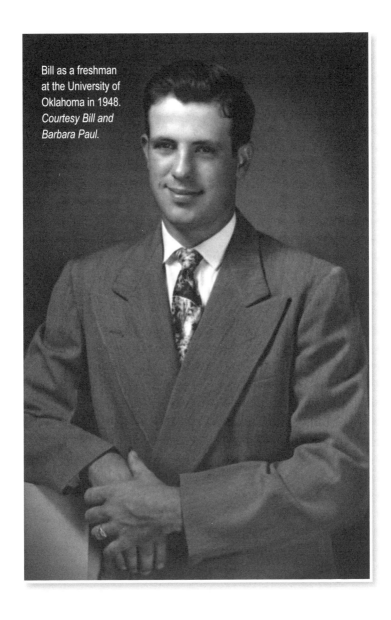

Bill as a freshman at the University of Oklahoma in 1948. *Courtesy Bill and Barbara Paul.*

COLLEGE—
AND FAMILY CRISIS

Willie's mother, Helen, was strong and instilled in her boys a unique
brand of integrity and always doing what was right.
—Judge Lee West

$\mathcal{F}$ollowing graduation from high school, Bill worked during
the summer on the family farm. He and his brother were
responsible for most of the chores and watching over the
alfalfa and small grain crops and 40 registered Hereford cattle
because their father was busy campaigning for re-election to
the State Senate.

Homer was trying to extend his legislative service for
another four years, but lost in a spirited campaign to Herbert
Hope of Maysville. Homer lost the race by 42 votes of more
than 8,000 votes cast. Homer was out of politics at the tender
age of 43. Trying to overcome the potential despair of being
dethroned as the "Robin Hood of the legislature," Homer
directed his efforts to his law practice and farming.[1]

During Bill's senior year in high school, he had
considered attending either of Oklahoma's two major

universities, Oklahoma Agricultural and Mechanical
College, now Oklahoma State University, in Stillwater or
the University of Oklahoma in Norman. He chose OU,
established December 19, 1890, by an act of the territorial
legislature.

When classes began at OU in September, 1892,
enrollment was simple. Each student met personally with
President Dr. David Ross Boyd to obtain a schedule and to be
quizzed by the faculty of four. A one-page sheet contained all
the courses offered by the university.

One of Bill's best friends in college was DeVier Pierson who perfected the hula
technique in preparation for a Phi Gamma Delta party. *Courtesy Bill and Barbara Paul.*

Bill and Bob Fields were introduced to the Greek fraternity system at OU and received a good rush from several different fraternities. They especially enjoyed the rush parties. In the end, both pledged Phi Gamma Delta and lived in the fraternity house their entire freshman year. Most of their social activities centered around the fraternity. There were blind dates, a Christmas party, a Fiji Island party, Sunday afternoon open houses, intramural sports, fraternity sings, formal dinners, and an annual football game, the Finger Bowl, against the boys from Sigma Alpha Epsilon.[2]

Bill's friends in the fraternity included Lee Allan Smith, Lee Stidham, Joe Cannon, Eddie Crowder, Charles Johnson, Chester Cadieux, Don Atkins, Jim Arnold, Charles Coleman, Dick Cain, Frank and Bill Robinson, and Jim Davis.

Other Phi Gamma Delta friends included Hardy Summers, Jack Catlett, DeVier Pierson, Bill Lockard, Joe and Dick Ellis, Bob Saunders, Lou Trost, Sam Wilson, Bill Rea, Jim Hart, Bill Beckman, Jim Gorman, John Drake, Jim Clowe, David Hall, Jim West, Dick Van Cleef, and Jack Godfrey. Bill's brother, Homer, also was a member of Phi Gamma Delta.

Using the lesson he had learned about test taking from Mrs. Carleton in high school, Bill studied to prepare for the entrance examination that was given to all incoming freshmen at OU. When he completed the exam, he believed he had done well. However, he forgot about the exam until he received word from his parents that OU President Dr. George L. Cross had called with the news that Bill had made the highest score ever recorded on an OU entrance examination.

A few weeks later, Dr. Cross and his wife visited the
fraternity house and asked to be introduced to Bill. They
were gracious in recognizing his accomplishment on the
entrance exam. It was the beginning of a long and wonderful
association with Dr. and Mrs. Cross during Bill's student days
at OU.[3]

At the time, OU freshmen male students were required
to enroll in the Reserve Officers Training Corps (ROTC)
program. Students had an option to join the Army, Navy, or
Air Force ROTC units. Bill applied for the Navy program
because it was rumored to be an elite group that took only 60
students a year. He did well on an aptitude test and passed
a rigorous physical examination and was accepted into the
Navy ROTC (NROTC) program.

Bill and other NROTC cadets were required to take a
course in naval science each semester and drill for two hours
every Tuesday afternoon. The faculty was brilliant. The drill
instructor was a tough Marine sergeant. The Professor of
Naval Science was a Navy captain, the executive officer was
a Navy commander. The first-year instructor was Lieutenant
Commander Hokr, a graduate of the United States Naval
Academy, a submarine officer, and a career Navy officer.
He taught Navy customs, history, nomenclature, military
courtesy, and military traditions.

Some of Bill's closest college friends were NROTC
classmates, including Lee West, Don Symcox, Sam Wilson,
Lee Jenkins, Pat Keenan, Bill Harrah, Jim Weatherall, Owen
Garriott, Phil Kidd, Jack Lockett, and Jim Clowe. West later
became chairman of the Civil Aeronautics Board and United

States District Judge for the Western District of Oklahoma. Jim Weatherall was a football star at OU and Garriott became an American astronaut. Symcox, who became a successful banker, identified with Bill because of a common heritage of being raised in a small town. Symcox said, "From the early times in NROTC, we knew Bill would be something special in life." [4]

NROTC was rewarding for Bill. He was chosen as the outstanding NROTC cadet for each of his four years at OU. In his senior year, he was student Battalion Commander. He began the year as second in command until the tragic death of Graham Johnson of Norman in an automobile accident. Other friends in the NROTC unit included Paul Lindsey, Mickey Imel, Tom Kenan, Dale Stauffer, Jim Hart, Gene Torbett, Dave Trapnell, John Dean, Paul Sprehe, and Jim Shanahan.

One of the fortuitous benefits of being a freshman at OU in 1948 was the presence on campus of World War II veterans using the GI Bill to further their education. The veterans were leaders in Bill's fraternity—they were serious students preparing themselves for careers. They were mature and disciplined. Under their leadership, fraternity house rules were strictly enforced, including a three-hour study period each week night.

Bill already was motivated to study. His normal routine was to study until midnight or later and get up just in time for class. Bill made straight As his first year and had the top score in every class except physics. In that class, which was required as part of the NROTC program, A.T. Stair, a physics major, took first place and Bill finished second. Ironically, three members of the small NROTC class are members of the Oklahoma Hall of Fame—Bill, Stair, and astronaut Owen Garriott.[5]

During Bill's freshman year, he developed a plan that he thought had great potential for improving relationships with and understanding international students. The plan involved fraternities awarding a room and board scholarship to an international student. Bill's fraternity was first to follow the plan, giving room and board to an Estonian, Ilmar Martens. The experience was rewarding to both the fraternity and Martens. Bill thought the idea might catch on and spread to other university campuses to create ambassadors of good will for America when the students returned to their home countries. The plan soon was abandoned but was resurrected 50 years later by OU President David L. Boren.[6]

Just before Thanksgiving, 1948, Bill's father was working in the barn feeding cattle when he fell into a manger and was injured. At first, it was thought that Homer had only broken a few ribs. However, he became very ill and was hospitalized. What was seemingly a minor injury developed into phlebitis, a condition of blood clots in his legs. With circulation greatly impaired, Homer grew worse. Doctors could not save him and he died on January 6, 1949, at the Pauls Valley General Hospital. It was a terribly sad and unexpected turn of events for the family.[7]

The death of Homer hit the Paul family hard. After the Sunday funeral, Bill returned to Norman in a bitter winter storm to begin final examinations the following morning. Bill,

Homer, Jr., and their mother had to formulate a plan to keep the family afloat. There was no indebtedness on the farm, but growing crops and raising beef and dairy cattle were the only sources of income. It was decided to make dairy farming the focus of the operation.

Homer, Jr. was a junior in high school and took on the major part of running the farm. Bill came home several times each month to help with farm chores and Helen worked from daylight to dark keeping the farm operation going. The dairy business increased. Homer, Jr. used milking machines to milk the cows, bottled the milk, and delivered milk in quart bottles to individuals in Pauls Valley in a pickup truck with a cab on back. He stopped by the ice plant and chopped up large blocks of ice to place on top of the milk to keep it fresh. He delivered the milk early in the mornings, seven days a week.[8]

When Homer, Jr. graduated from high school and enrolled at OU, Helen hired a farmhand to help with chores six days a week. Bill and Homer, Jr. came home on weekends to help.

Transportation to and from OU always was a problem for Bill. The farm pickup was needed for daily delivery of milk and Helen needed the family car. Sometimes Bill rode the bus from Norman to Pauls Valley, but the service was not always reliable. He often hitchhiked the 40-mile route going home or returning to school. On one occasion, he was picked up by one of his sports heroes, OU lineman Norman McNabb, and driven to Pauls Valley. McNabb was famous for recovering a fumble and scoring a touchdown for the 1946 Sooners when they almost defeated Army, the nation's top-ranked team.[9]

Except for his father's death, Bill's freshman year at OU was a magnificent experience. He made only As, was active in several campus organizations, was selected as the outstanding freshman in his fraternity, and received the Pe-et Award as the outstanding freshman student on the entire campus. Bill was featured in President Cross' column in *Sooner Magazine*. Cross mentioned Bill's program for helping bridge the cultural gap with international students and called Bill perhaps the most outstanding freshman to ever attend OU. Dr. Cross wrote:

> *"Willie" Paul is not a one sided personality. He is definitely not a bookworm. He has continued his athletic interests and took active part in the intramural sports program at OU. He took part also in an astonishing number of other extracurricular activities...*
>
> *In any university the size of this one, the competition for a good grades is fast and furious, and it is a very rare occasion when a student goes through a year without earning a single hour of credit with a grade lower than A, but is rarer still when this record is made by a student in his freshman year. It is an amazing achievement for a freshman to make this record while participating extensively in extracurricular activities and, at the same time, carrying much of the responsibility of managing a farm located nearly 50 miles from the campus. His first year record has been equaled only once in the history of the University.*[10]

Bill spent the summer of 1949 on the family farm, working in the fields and the dairy. Because alfalfa was harvested in the summer months, it was possible for much of the year's farm work to be accomplished without interfering with college classes. The first cutting of hay was in May but Helen hired local ranchers to help her with that. For the remainder of the summer, Bill and Homer, Jr. lifted the 70-pound bales of hay onto a truck and stacked it in the barns to be stored until higher prices could be obtained in the winter. Baling hay was hot, hard work.[11]

During Bill's sophomore year at OU, he moved to what was referred to as the fraternity "annex." He took his meals at the fraternity house, one block away, where room priority was for the freshman pledge class and upper classmen. Bill's roommate, however, was Oklahoma City freshman, DeVier Pierson, who later completed law school and became a successful lawyer in Washington, D.C. Pierson, who later worked for President Lyndon Johnson, said, "Willie was not only my roommate and friend, he was my mentor. He already was a leader. Even at age 20 he stood out as an example of leadership." [12]

Part of Bill's positive impact upon young students such as Pierson came from Bill's insistence that freshmen develop good study habits. "He made me understand early," Pierson remembered, "how important it was to have a good academic record. He made it clear that with a proper study protocol, it also was possible to have a good college social life." [13] Because of Bill's exposure to politics through his father's career and his own unique interest in government and leadership, Bill began participating in public speaking, or forensic activities at OU. He won first place in a campus oratory contest and successfully tried out for the varsity debate team. After two years in the OU debate program, he was inducted as a member of Delta Sigma Rho, an honorary forensic society.[14]

Debate was one of Bill's most exciting experiences at OU. He was proud to represent his school at debate contests—it was a great educational opportunity. University debaters always were furnished a national question that they had to be prepared to argue for or against. In Bill's sophomore year, the question was, "Should the basic industries of the United States be nationalized?" To prepare for the topic, Bill spent a lot of time in the business school library learning about the nation's demographics, the gross national product, the federal budget, the size of the national debt, and per capita income.[15]

Bill made lifelong friends on the debate team. E. Deane Kanaly of Oklahoma City later founded a very successful trust company based in Houston, Texas. Kanaly remembered, "It was quite an experience to ride trains to tournaments in Iowa, Texas, and other surrounding states. We sharpened our debate skills en route by playing long chess matches." Kanaly died in 2006.[16]

Other debate partners were Owen Garriott of Enid, Oklahoma, an engineering student who later became the first civilian astronaut in space as a crew member of Sky Lab I, and James A. Peabody of Oklahoma City. Peabody later was one of Bill's law partners.

In Bill's junior year, the debate topic was, "Resolved that the communist party of the United States should be outlawed." The topic was timely in 1950-1951 because some people in America believed there was a communist lurking behind every rock in the land. Bill and Peabody won every match that year except for one against the University of Arkansas. The Arkansas plan was to lynch all communists, to string them up from lamp posts. The OU response was to ridicule such an outlandish proposal. The judges ruled against Bill and Peabody on the basis that ridicule was never a proper strategy in debate.[17]

One of the most memorable debate trips was to Iowa City, Iowa, on a frozen University of Iowa campus. The meet was held in the former State Senate chamber of a beautiful building that once had served as the capitol of Iowa. OU had little money and the debate team operated on a bare bones budget. The team traveled to Iowa on a milk train that stopped every ten miles to pick up milk cans.[18]

During the fall semester of Bill's junior year, he began dating Mary-Lynn Cross, the daughter of the OU president and Mrs. Cross. The Crosses encouraged and supported Bill's academic endeavors and often invited him to their home. Dr. Cross invited Bill to attend the Sugar Bowl game in New Orleans, Louisiana, on New Year's Day, 1951. The two flew with corporate executives on a Phillips Petroleum Company airplane, quite an experience for a young farm boy from Pauls Valley. Bill's seatmate on the trip to New Orleans was Paul Endacott, a friendly man with whom Bill chatted for hours. At the end of the conversation, Bill asked Endacott what his position was with Phillips. Endacott kindly replied, "Well, at one time or another, I've done about everything there is to do—but just now I'm the president." Endacott was so unassuming that Bill never realized he was the president of the giant oil concern.[19]

What was intended to be a one-day trip to the Sugar Bowl turned into a three-day adventure. Torrential rains grounded the company plane in New Orleans. With no luggage, fresh clothing, or a shaving kit, Bill shared a room with President Cross. Bill described the time as "a unique opportunity to become closely acquainted with an outstanding man." [20]

FLYING AND CRUISING

I neglected to calculate the effect of the rotation of the earth.
—Bill Paul

Another great college experience for Bill was learning to fly in 1951 in the OU aviation program. The basic aviation course allowed students 40 hours of flying time and graduation with a private pilot's license. Somehow, Bill scraped enough money together to pay the extra tuition for the training. He loved the lessons in the university's four Aeronca Champion aircraft. However, Oklahoma winds sometimes played havoc with schedules. If the wind was greater than 30 miles-per-hour, the planes were grounded.

One of the highlights of the aviation training was OU's hosting of the National Intercollegiate Flying Association meet. Aviation teams from two dozen colleges and universities flew into Norman's Westheimer Field. One of the events of the competition involved using navigation skills. Young pilots were given a map on which a triangular flight course was drawn. They had to fly the course and estimate the flight time.

The faculty had pre-flown the courses and developed a set of questions. No timekeeping devices were allowed and students were asked a series of questions to make certain they had flown the course. The contestant who came closest to his or her estimated time was the winner.

Bill had been studying navigation in the NROTC program under the watchful eye of a naval aviator, Lieutenant Commander V.L. Michaeel, a graduate of Iowa State University, from whom Bill got some helpful tutoring in preparation for the event. Bill meticulously estimated the flight time of the predetermined contest route. He calculated the velocity and direction of the wind on the ground and at various altitude levels and the speed at which he would fly the route.

Bill was the only contestant to turn in a time that was down to a specific second. His time was one hour, eleven minutes, and ten seconds. Bill completed the course and set a national record by being only one second off. He received some good natured ribbing from other contestants who wondered how he could be a whole second off. Bill replied, "I neglected to calculate the effect of the rotation of the earth."

Bill was so close to the actual flight time that his regular flight instructor sought him out and asked him to explain how he made the precise calculation. Later Bill discovered the instructor was asked to inquire because meet officials could not explain the accuracy of Bill's estimate without a watch or other illegal timekeeping device. After the explanation, the officials were satisfied that Bill had won the event fair and square.[1]

A highlight of Bill's junior year in Norman was being elected to the Pe-et Society, a unique campus organization composed of the ten outstanding men in the junior class. Others included Fred Harris of Lawton, who later became United States Senator from Oklahoma and who has continued to be a close friend of Bill's. Two fraternity brothers, David Hall of Oklahoma City and Sam Wilson of Norman, the top graduate in the OU engineering school, also became members of the Society. Hall was later governor of Oklahoma and Wilson founded a very successful company based in Austin, Texas. Another member of the Society was Bill's friend, Reford Bond, of Chickasha, who became a distinguished lawyer.

When the ten men met for an organizational meeting, Harris nominated Bill as Society president. On the first ballot, Bill and another member tied, 5-5. The second ballot was identical. On the third ballot, Bill's opponent nominated one

The officers of the Pe-et Society in 1952, left to right, Fred Harris, Dexter Eldridge, David Hall, Dean Earl Sneed, Jr., Bill, Jim Miller, and Bill Price. *Courtesy Bill and Barbara Paul.*

of Bill's friends as a third candidate. When the votes were counted, Bill had four votes, his opponent had five votes, and the new candidate garnered one vote.

Society president Ted Webb of Fort Worth, Texas, was about to declare Bill's opponent the victor but decided to review the group's by-laws. He found that a majority vote was needed and Bill's opponent had received only five of ten votes. On a final vote, Bill again was nominated and won the election 6-4. He never knew who had changed his vote in the secret ballot.[2]

The Pe-et Society had for some time presented an award to the outstanding male in the freshman class, an honor that Bill received two years before. Under Bill's leadership nine additional freshmen men were recognized as the "freshman top ten." It was the Society's hope that male freshmen would aspire to be included and recognized as top students in their class.

During the summer before Bill's senior year at OU, he was required to take a NROTC "cruise." Part of the agreement for receiving a Naval Reserve commission at the end of NROTC training was participation in a four-week cruise. However, because the Korean War was in progress in the summer of 1951, the Navy decided to combine the shorter cruise for its contract students such as Bill with scholarship students who to receive a regular Navy commission normally had an eight-week cruise. The combined cruise was six weeks.

Bill was assigned to the USS Missouri, the World War II battleship that General Douglas MacArthur made famous by accepting the formal surrender of the Japanese on its top

Bill, as a Midshipman First Class, sends a message by blinker light about the battleship USS Missouri during a Naval Reserve Officer Training Corps training cruise. *Courtesy Bill and Barbara Paul.*

deck. Bill and other NROTC midshipmen boarded the ship at Norfolk, Virginia. After spending two days in New York City, the ship, flanked by three destroyers, sailed to the Panama Canal, stopped at Guantanamo Bay, Cuba, and returned to Norfolk.[3]

During the navigation, engineering, and gunnery training, Bill became well acquainted with Lee West. He had known West in NROTC, but they were never close friends until the 1951 cruise. West likewise believed the summer cruise began a lifetime friendship with Bill. West said, "I never knew anyone who instinctively wanted to do what was right more than Willie. He has been an inspiration to me over the decades. Everything he did, he wanted to be the best, and wanted everyone around him to excel." [4]

Another constant companion on the cruise was Lee Jenkins. After each day's training, Bill, West, and Jenkins got together on deck and entertained themselves.

The only negative of the cruise came when Bill injured his right knee. The ship's doctor referred Bill for evaluation to the United States Navy hospital at Norfolk. After three days of diagnostic tests, it was determined that Bill had just sprained his knee. He was released to return home to the farm at Pauls Valley.[5]

OU offered a combined degree program at the time which allowed Bill to complete his undergraduate degree at the same time he took classes as a freshman in the OU College of Law. It shortened school time for aspiring lawyers from seven to six years. Later Bill questioned his decision to hurry the process. If he could have afforded an additional year, he perhaps would have used his fourth undergraduate year to concentrate on arts and sciences and defer his entry into the law school. He discovered being a serious law student was a full-time endeavor and required as much maturity as possible.[6]

Since the age of 10 or 11, Bill had wanted to be a lawyer. He respected his father's profession and believed his forensics training would equip him for a strong career in the law. He also looked up to his uncle, Haskell Paul, a seasoned lawyer and judge.

Bill had many diversions during his first year of law school. He helped his mother and brother on the family farm, he was student commander of the NROTC battalion, president of the Pe-et Society, active in his fraternity, and had become engaged to Mary-Lynn Cross. Bill lived in a garage apartment at President Cross' house. The rent was reasonable and he was conveniently located near classes and his fiancé.

Bill's roommate was Jack Gardner of McAlester, Oklahoma. In addition to becoming good friends with Gardner, Bill spent a lot of time with Lee West and Lee Jenkins, both in NROTC and in law school, studying together. Bill also invited them to the family farm on some weekends.

Two of Bill's friends vied for the position of president of the OU law school freshman class. Bill nominated and backed Lee West for the job. West won. Bill's other good friend, Fred Harris, was elected vice president.

Bill was impressed with the quality of instruction at the OU College of Law. The law school had admitted its first students in 1909. The first dean was Julien C. Monnet, a graduate of Harvard University. Monnet, who served until 1941, made the law school progressive and assembled a faculty from the leading law schools of the nation. An exceptional library became a boast. The school became a model for other law schools throughout the country. Monnet's graduates, many of whom became leaders in the state and nation, were referred to as the Dean's "boys." [7]

Among law school professors who gained Bill's admiration were Victor Culp, an outstanding national authority on oil and gas law; Eugene Kuntz, who succeeded Dr. Culp; Maurice Merrill, a nationally-recognized constitutional law scholar; and Olin Browder, who moved on to the University of Michigan and became a renowned teacher of property law.[8]

Bill not only appreciated the quality of the law school, but enjoyed the national prominence of the OU football team.

Charles "Bud" Wilkinson had become head coach in the 1947 season at age 33 and began a great tradition of winning. In his second year, Wilkinson took the Sooners to the Sugar Bowl and beat the University of North Carolina. From that point forward, Oklahoma University became one of the most successful college football programs. In fact, since World War II, OU has the best winning percentage among major colleges.

Although he performed reasonably well, Bill did not finish near the top of his freshman law school class. His friend, Fred Harris, held that richly-deserved honor. Bill was impressed with Harris' efforts. He said, "Fred had one of the keenest intellects of anyone I have ever known." [9]

The Naval Reserve Officers' Training Corps officers at OU in 1952. Front row, left to right, Bill, G.B. Johnson, who was killed in an automobile crash a few months later, P.D. Kenan, and S.A. Wilson. Back row, David C. Zimmerman, John H. Siegmund, and R.E. McCamey. *Courtesy Bill and Barbara Paul.*

In early 1952, Bill, along with his friends, West and Jenkins, opted to take his reserve commission in the United States Marine Corps, rather than the United States Navy. Part of the reason the three wanted to become Marines was the persuasion of Lieutenant Colonel Gerry Russell, the Marine officer who served as an instructor in the NROTC program at OU. Russell was a "fantastic recruiter" and talked Bill, West, and Jenkins into taking their commissions in the Marine Corps.

Another reason Bill wanted to be a Marine was because the corps was an elite group. The war in Korea had been raging since the summer of 1950 when North Korea invaded South Korea and the United States intervened. Bill knew that he would be called to active duty when he received his undergraduate degree and his Marine Corps commission in May, 1952.

What made entrance into the Marine Corps even more attractive was the promise that the first six months of active duty would be spent in new officer training at The Basic School at Quantico, Virginia, a nice venue for military service.

After shifting to the Marine program, Bill's NROTC course in the spring semester of 1952 was the study of the history, organization, weaponry, and mission of the Corps. He remembered, "I became excited about becoming a Marine, but it was all in the books for me as I had not yet worn the uniform, even for a day, and had not yet fired any of the weapons." [10]

Lieutenant Colonel Gerry Russell was Bill's Marine Officer instructor at OU. *Courtesy Bill and Barbara Paul.*

Bill's senior year of undergraduate school came to a busy and rushed conclusion. He was selected as the recipient of the Letzseiser Gold Medal as the outstanding male graduate in the senior class. He was presented the outstanding male graduate award by the Rotary Club of Norman and, for the fourth consecutive year, was named the outstanding NROTC student in his class. He also was inducted into membership in Phi Beta Kappa.[11]

The first week of June, 1952, was an eventful one. Bill received his Bachelor of Arts degree from OU, was commissioned a second lieutenant in the United States Marine Corps Reserve, received his orders to two years active duty, and was married to Mary-Lynn Cross.

ESPRIT de CORPS

After another young Marine dropped dead on the first day of basic training, I wondered, "Am I going to be tough enough for this?"
—Bill Paul

After a June honeymoon in Colorado and working on the family farm for a few weeks, Bill and Mary-Lynn left for Quantico, Virginia, in mid-July, 1952. They did not own an automobile, so they borrowed Dr. Cross' 1946 Packard for the trip. Already in Virginia were Lee West and Lee Jenkins who, as regular officers, had been ordered to active duty earlier in the summer.

All three friends were in the same training class, the 15th Special Basic Course, in which they were trained as infantry platoon leaders. It was part of the Marine philosophy that every Marine is a rifleman, although basic training was followed with special military occupational training.[1]

Soon after arriving in Virginia, Bill, West, and Jenkins discovered that Lieutenant Colonel Russell had oversold the Quantico experience. Instead of being quartered in the lovely, old colonial-style brick buildings on the main part of the base along the Potomac River, they were housed 12 miles away at Camp Barrett, a collection of sheet metal Quonset huts. The single officers stayed in the Quonset huts. The married officers had a bunk and locker there, but actually spent their nights in rented housing in the area surrounding Quantico. The commute to Camp Barrett made for long training days.[2]

Bill's first day on active duty was hot, humid, and memorable. He stood in line in his skivvies with 20 or 30 other second lieutenants for a physical examination. All was calm until Bill saw a commotion in the hallway with several hospital attendants running and pushing a gurney with a body on it. A few minutes later, word was passed that a Marine had passed out on the drill field and died. Bill's first thought was, "Am I going to be tough enough for this?" The following day, the Marine Corps remedied the situation and mandated that outdoor drills would be canceled if the temperature and relative humidity exceeded certain limits.[3]

Because of the manpower demands of the Korean War, the Marine basic training course had been compressed from nine months to five and half months. Bill had to play catch-up in the first few weeks because he reported as a second lieutenant without even a single day of military training, except for the six weeks on the cruise in the Atlantic Ocean. Most other officers had spent a summer of training and were at least familiar with the Marines' basic weapon, the M-1 rifle.

Bill was issued an M-1 and was taught from his first day on duty to care for his weapon as if his life depended on it. For Marines in combat, that lesson was true. Bill and other trainees were instructed how to disassemble the M-1 piece-by-piece, clean it, and put it together again.

Bill's first experience at standing in the ranks and being inspected was not a pleasant one. Bill stood in platoon formation and was expected to open the bolt of his rifle for inspection as a captain approached him. Bill watched others in the line before him, but failed to recognize that he was supposed to hand the rifle to the inspecting captain with one hand. When Bill used both hands to present the rifle, the captain said with some amazement, "Well, lieutenant, I know it's easier to hold that rifle with both hands—but we don't do it that way!" [4]

Bill's training class was made up of 550 graduates of the NROTC program, the United States Naval Academy, and the Officers Candidate School. Most, like Bill, were reserve officers. There was no distinction between regular and reserve officers in training—they were all Marines. But there was some difference in motivation. Many of the regulars intended to pursue a military career and approached training with serious dedication. [5]

The Marine instructors were Korean War veterans—most had recently returned from active duty in the war zone. Their job was to teach trainees to lead a Marine platoon in the Korean combat environment. By that time, the war front had stabilized and most of the action involved leading patrols or probes in front of the line or defending the line from entrenched positions against enemy attacks. Much of the war action was at night so instruction concentrated on night operations.

Training was as realistic as possible. Instructors

mimicked actions of Chinese and North Korean troops on the front in Korea. Trainees were placed in a defensive position on a hill and after nightfall an attack was mounted. Instructors used jeeps equipped with loudspeakers in an effort to frighten the trainees by booming out messages such as, "Marine, tonight you die!" [6]

Marine training was a combination of classroom and field exercises. Bill and fellow trainees spent many hours on the drill field and running the obstacle course. The training was less strenuous than for enlisted Marines, but Bill's physical condition was greatly enhanced.

The most strenuous outdoor activity was a 20-mile hike, with weapons and full packs, at night following a full day of activity. For eight hours, the Marines averaged hiking two and one half miles per hour. They marched for 50 minutes and rested for ten minutes. Bill said, "We all made it, but we were a bunch of tired second lieutenants when we got in!" [7]

Free time provided great travel opportunities for Bill and his friends. Washington, D.C., was only a half hour from the base. Many historic places such as Civil War battlefields were only a short drive away. At Thanksgiving in 1952, Bill and Mary-Lynn drove with Lee West and his new bride, Mary Ann, to New York City. They returned through Philadelphia and attended the Army-Navy football game. They, of course, rooted for Navy. They were intrigued by the public address announcer's comment, "Admiral Brown, would you move your battleship? It is blocking traffic in the Delaware." The announcement was a reference to the Delaware River on which the Port of Philadelphia and Philadelphia Navy Yard were located.[8]

Bill and West were huge OU football fans and followed the Sooners from afar. Bill's friend and fraternity brother, Eddie Crowder, was the OU quarterback, and it was the year halfback Billy Vessels won the Heisman Trophy, the most coveted award in college football.

OU played Notre Dame that season and Bill and West accepted the invitation of Notre Dame graduate, George O'Tott, to watch the game on television at his home. Although OU lost the game, Vessels was very impressive in his performance before a national television audience and perhaps started the momentum for his winning the Heisman Trophy.

On another weekend, Bill and West drove to College Park, Maryland, to watch the University of Maryland play football. Maryland was coached by "Sunny" Jim Tatum who had coached the OU football team and brought Bud Wilkinson to Norman. Tatum was thought by many to have been the initial architect of Oklahoma's national prominence in football. Bill liked one of Tatum's quotes, "Winning isn't just important—it's all that matters!" [9]

Bill's Marine training ended with what was called a "three-day war." It was a field exercise of three days and two nights in the field, putting into practice the principles learned during the previous five months. The trainees were placed in the middle of the forest on the large Marine base around Quantico. There was an abundance of creeks and "runs" carrying water to the Potomac River.

What Bill learned quickly was how difficult it was to maintain coordination and control when in an unfriendly environment. It was hard to know where he was, where the adjacent units were, where the objective was, and the location of mock enemy units. Bill rotated with other students in platoon leader, platoon sergeant, or squad leader positions.

During his training time at Quantico, Bill developed a great love and respect for the Marine Corps. He always has been proud of being a Marine and believes in the slogan, "Once a Marine, always a Marine." Even before Bill left for training, he knew the pride of being a Marine. Wray Loftin was a family friend and neighbor in Pauls Valley who had served as a combat Marine in World War I. Bill could see pride swell in Loftin's eyes when he said, "Son, I'm glad you're going to be a Marine. When I was a Marine, they made the ships out of wood and the men out of steel."

Bill learned first hand the meaning of "esprit de corps." Bill said, "Because of the leadership, training, history, and the example set by Marines before me, I developed a feeling that I had to do my duty because others were counting on me. I also had the confidence that my fellow Marines would do their duty. If I was ever in a tight spot, in harm's way, I would choose to be with a fellow Marine." [10]

Near the end of The Basic School, in December, 1952, Bill was asked to express a preference for assignment to a military occupation specialty. He requested artillery, infantry, and tanks—in that order. When he received his assignment, however, it was in the Marine Air Wing. Even though he was not given his preference, he was delighted with his duty.

Bill's class graduated just before Christmas. After a few days home in Oklahoma, he reported to his duty station at the El Toro Marine Corps Air Station (El Toro) at Irvine,

California. He arranged for an advance on his pay and bought the 1946 Packard from Dr. Cross. It was Bill's first car and served him until the end of law school.

El Toro, now inactive, was Marine aviation headquarters on the West Coast. A Marine Air Wing is the equivalent of an Army division and is made up of Marine Air Groups, the same as an Army regiment. Bill was attached to an Air Group that was housed at the nearby Santa Ana Marine Corps Air Facility, a small airfield from which several helicopter squadrons and a Navy blimp squadron operated. The Navy had two huge blimps that were housed in two gargantuan hangars.[11]

At the time, the area around the two military installations in Orange County, California, still was lightly populated. The asphalt roads were lined with eucalyptus trees with silver leaves and a nice fragrance filled the air. Well-tended orange groves, soybean fields, and pastureland dotted the landscape. Now, the Irvine area is one of the wealthiest areas in the nation and is stacked with commercial buildings, shopping centers, and housing developments. The orange groves and pastures are gone.[12]

The mission of Bill's squadron was to support Marine aviation in the conduct of amphibious operations. He and his fellow Marines used mobile radar and communications equipment to conduct air defense surveillance operations, to control Marine fighters to intercept and destroy enemy aircraft, and to assist in airfield management.

Two maneuvers dominated the ten months training. In February, 1953, more than 200 men and officers and equipment were airlifted by flying boxcars, R4Qs, into the Mojave Desert to establish a camp and set up operations. It was like building a small town—but it had to be done in 24 hours. A mess tent with a portable kitchen, a medical dispensary, operation tents, and sleeping facilities had to be constructed.[13]

The second maneuver was an amphibious exercise. The idea was to come ashore on the coast of the Pacific Ocean at Camp Pendleton, about 40 miles south of El Toro. However, because most Navy ships were busy in the Korean War, Bill and his fellow Marines "came ashore" in trucks, rather than land in regular landing craft, LST's. The unit's orders were to make a beach landing in "LST 101," a reference to the California Highway 101 on which the Marines arrived by truck.

Bill's only problem during the landing maneuver was a bad sunburn. While off duty on the beautiful California beach, he decided to remove his shirt and take in the sun. He fell asleep and was badly sunburned on his back. When he reported to medical, a Navy corpsman asked how the sunburn had occurred. When Bill told him the truth, the corpsman said, "Lieutenant, if you turn yourself in for treatment, you should know that it is a court martial offense to get a sunburn except in the line of duty." Bill said he immediately felt better and did not need medical help.[14]

One of Bill's duties in his Marine squadron was to serve as enlisted training officer. The unit had about 200 enlisted men, mostly technicians who operated, repaired, and maintained the squadron's electronic equipment. As training officer, Bill's job was to make certain the enlisted men maintained competency in basic military skills. He periodically inspected the troops on the drill field in full combat packs. There was minimal marching drill and occasional trips to the firing range.

Bill also conducted classroom training on personal hygiene, military courtesy, discipline, and amphibious warfare tactics. Once he accompanied his trainees on a 20-mile hike from the Marine facility at Santa Ana to an auxiliary airfield, Palisades, ten miles away. Because there were no full packs or weapons and was made in the middle of a gorgeous California day, the trek was not as strenuous as Bill had experienced at Quantico.[15]

Approximately half the officers in Bill's squadrons were pilots who had to fly a minimum number of hours each month to qualify for flight pay. Ground officers such as Bill often hitched rides on the military aircraft. It was especially thrilling because he was a civilian pilot.

On one trip, Bill and another officer accompanied a pilot on a trip down the California coast in a TBM, a World War II torpedo bomber. The scenery was marvelous and the trip was uneventful until the return to base. Bill donned headsets and heard radio traffic talking about an aircraft that was having problems getting its landing gear down. Only when the TBM passed over the control tower did Bill realize the plane in trouble was his. He was in the belly of the plane that would skid along the runway if the landing gear would not deploy. Observers in the control tower said the gear appeared to be down and that surely the problem was the cockpit indicator light. However, to prepare for the worst, emergency vehicles lined the runway as the aircraft made a normal landing. The trouble was a bad indicator light bulb.[16]

In June, 1953, Bill made his first trip to Hawaii for a month-long training period. He was assigned to Barbers Point, one of the best Navy air control training facilities available to the Marine Corps. After an arduous, 20-hour flight from Oakland, California, to Hawaii aboard a slow, four-engine "flying boat," Bill arrived in Hawaii eight years before it became a state.

Barbers Point Naval Air Station was about 20 miles from Honolulu and was located on the coast. The drive between Honolulu and Barbers Point was breathtaking. Sugar cane fields and sugar mills lined the road. Majestic mountains rose beyond the fields.

Daily training sessions usually ended about 3:00 p.m. so there was plenty of time for sightseeing and recreation. Bill and several other officers bought an old car for $50 to drive to Honolulu and Waikiki Beach. While in Hawaii, Bill visited his fraternity brother and NROTC classmate, Sam Wilson, a Navy ensign assigned to a ship based at Pearl Harbor. Bill also looked up another Quantico classmate, Dick Hopper.

Waikiki Beach was not as developed as it is today. There were two major hotels on the strip, the Royal Hawaiian, called the Pink Palace, and the Moana, which had a huge Banyan tree in the courtyard located on the pristine beach. One night, Bill met actor Lee Marvin in the courtyard. Marvin, in Hawaii filming "The Caine Mutiny," had served as an enlisted man in the Marine Corps in World War II and enjoyed stories from Korean-era Marines.[17]

While Bill was on duty in Hawaii, the Armistice was signed, ending the Korean War and establishing the 38th parallel to separate the two Koreas. When he returned to California, his duty assignment was the same. Even though the Armistice had been signed, the American military continued to maintain the same level of forces in South Korea. Officers from Bill's squadron were rotated for duty in Korea. Bill assumed he would be sent to the war-torn region soon.

When Bill and Mary-Lynn were married, she had completed only three years of college at OU. So with the threat of Bill heading for South Korea, Mary-Lynn returned to Norman to complete her bachelor's degree. She drove the Packard back to Oklahoma, leaving Bill without transportation and "glued" to the base.[18]

Bill was stationed in South Korea as a Marine officer in 1954.
Courtesy Bill and Barbara Paul.

Even though the Korean people were energetic and innovative, they
suffered greatly from decades of Japanese domination.
—Bill Paul

*I*n December, 1953, Bill was designated company commander
for the group of Marines preparing for assignment in South
Korea. Once they arrived on the peninsula, the company would
be disbanded and the individual Marines would head for
specific assignments. For the 30 days Bill was the "company
commander," he depended upon his Marine master sergeant to
keep the 200 Marines under control.

When it was time to leave for South Korea, Bill led his
troops by train to San Diego, California, marched them five
blocks to the Navy pier, and boarded the USS Ulysses S.
Grant, a military sea transport. The vessel looked like a Navy
ship but was operated by a civilian captain and crew. Bill's
unit joined another 1,000 Marines headed for duty in South
Korea or Japan.[1]

On the smooth, 17-day trip across the Pacific Ocean, Bill slept in cramped quarters—four Marine officers in two double bunks in a small cabin. The ship dropped anchor in Kobe Bay, Japan, where Bill saw the Japanese sunrise and marveled at the land of which he had only read in books. When the ship docked at the port, Bill said goodbye to his troops who were sent in different directions. Bill went to Itami Air Field, a Marine air base in the southern section of Honshu Island. It was a staging area for transportation to South Korea.

Bill and fellow Marines assigned to the First Marine Air Wing Headquarters flew on another flying boxcar from Itami to K-9 Airfield at Pohang, a small village on the east coast of South Korea. Korean airfields were numbered rather than given special names. The airfield was a Japanese base during the time Japan occupied Korea and had been expanded and modernized by the Marine Corps. Bill was assigned to an Air Control Group, was promoted to first lieutenant, and became a watch officer in the communications center.[2]

The accommodations at K-9 were excellent. Bill lived in a metal Quonset hut with running water. Quonset huts also housed an officers' club and a mess hall. Navy Seabees had erected a large wooden water tower that supplied running water to most of the base. Fifty years later, Bill discovered that William "Bill" Swisher, founder of Oklahoma City's CMI Corporation, was one of the Seabees who built the water tower. Several large diesel generators provided somewhat unreliable electricity for K-9 which was home to three Marine Air Groups, including night fighter aircraft, photo air reconnaissance, helicopter, and transport aircraft squadrons.

After returning from the Marines in the summer of 1954, Bill pitched in on the hot job of hauling hay on the Paul dairy farm near Pauls Valley. *Courtesy Bill and Barbara Paul.*

A part of the Marines' mission at K-9 was air defense. Chinese and North Korean pilots were infamous for playing a game—flying to the 38th parallel and abruptly turning around and then flying north. The problem was that American forces never knew which aircraft might keep coming, making it necessary to scramble air defense fighter aircraft. After awhile, the game became mundane, increasing the risk that American observers might become complacent.[3]

Occasionally, Bill accompanied pilots in his squadron. On his first flight in a jet, Bill flew up the west coast of South Korea almost to the 38th parallel, across the Korean peninsula, and returned to K-9. Bill sat in the seat normally occupied by the radar operator, but had no idea how to operate the equipment.

There was a lot of free time for Marines stationed at K-9. Bill read and played many games of volleyball and ping pong. The base was 200 miles south of the 38th parallel and was relatively safe. Often Bill checked out a jeep from the motor pool and visited nearby Korean villages where people lived in huts with thatched roofs.

Most of the locals were farmers or fishermen who either went barefoot or wore rubber sandals. Even though the people were industrious, they still suffered from decades of Japanese occupation. The village of Pohang where Bill was stationed three decades later became the headquarters of Pohang Steel. The modern steel mill is a sharp contrast to the village that Bill knew.[4]

Bill on a tour of rest and relaxation in Japan in 1954. He earned the "R and R" after several months duty in South Korea. *Courtesy Bill and Barbara Paul.*

After several months duty in South Korea, Bill earned a
period of rest and relaxation in Japan. He returned to Itami
Air Field and visited the sites in the Kobe-Osaka-Kyoto area.
One memorable day trip was to the old Imperial capital of
Japan that was filled with beautiful buildings and gardens
with wide boulevards. Bill took the time to visit shops,
looking at silk fabrics, and absorbing as much of the Japanese
culture as he could in a short visit.

He was especially impressed with Japanese school
children who wore uniforms, were well disciplined, and
behaved well in public. He was equally intrigued by the
appearance of many people wearing masks, trying to prevent
the spread of disease among so many people living in a small
area. For cultural enrichment, Bill attended a performance at
the Takaraska Opera, made famous by author James Michener
and Hollywood in films about the Korean War era in Japan.
All the performers were women—even male roles were
played by women.[5]

To occupy time in the officers' club back at K-9, Marines
sang songs. A few of them were rather bawdy, but all were
clever. One refrain Bill remembers is:

When the ice is on the rice in southern Honshu
And the sake in the cellar starts to freeze
And you whisper to your Jo-San [Japanese girlfriend]
  "I adore you"
Then you're going just a skoshe [little bit] Nipponese.

Many of the songs sung by Marines in the Air Wing
had to do with the risky business in which the pilots were
engaged. To understand one song, it was necessary to know
there were 24 aircraft in a squadron. This song is about a pilot

who flew a very risky night mission and went down, never to
return. Bill remembers the first two lines:

Twas a dark and stormy night
Not a star in sight

Then the refrain described the mission and getting shot
down. The final two lines were:

Tell the skipper for me
That he now has 23.

Bill took advantage of his time in South Korea to take
many photographs. He bought his first camera at the base
exchange. He paid $84, a small fortune at the time, for a
small German-made camera, a Contessa. He used the camera
for the next 25 years and it still works well.[6]

Bill became well acquainted with a young Korean boy
named Kim who worked in a civilian job at K-9. He was
18 or 19 years old, spoke good English, and seemed to be
extremely intelligent. For awhile, Bill wanted to bring Kim to
the United States to attend college. Bill made some effort to
make that happen, but plans never gelled to do so.

Kim had a unique way of communicating ideas. When
Bill asked him how it was living under Japanese control,
Kim said the problem was that his people were taught how
to tell time but not taught how to make a watch. It was a
commentary on the oppression Korean people endured during
the long Japanese occupation.

In the middle of the assignment in South Korea, Bill's
group commander tried to convince him to make the Marine
Corps his career. He was informed he had been approved for
retention and that his reserve commission could be changed

to a regular commission. Bill told his commander that he valued and treasured his experience in the Marine Corps, but he still wanted to be a lawyer in Oklahoma.[7]

In a sense, Bill began his legal career in the Marine Corps. At that time, non-lawyers could serve as both prosecutors and defense counsel in special courts martial that involved a trial before a panel of three officers for violations of the Uniform Code of Military Justice. The special courts martial had limited authority over the severity of punishment.

Bill began acting as defense counsel. One of his cases involved defending a young Marine who obviously had a low IQ and was accused of sleeping at his post. In preparing the case, Bill discovered the young man could not read. When Bill put him on the witness stand, he asked his client if he had received any oral instructions or orders about his duties. He answered no. The prosecution was based upon the idea that general orders, including the admonition to stay awake, are posted in various places and all military personnel are required to follow them.

Then Bill handed the defendant a comic book and asked him to read it to the Court. He admitted he could not read the book. Bill's defense that the young man could not follow general orders because he could not read them failed, but it was a nice try and the officers gave only minor punishment.

On another occasion Bill defended a sergeant from New York who was charged with being discourteous by insulting a superior officer. Bill's client was not a model Marine but had insulted a major who many considered to be the most unpopular human on the base. No one liked him.

Bill's trial tactic was based upon the small population of K-9—surely the trial officers knew of the major's poor reputation. So rather than to defend the action, Bill went on the offense and "tried" the major who was the chief prosecution witness. Bill's client was acquitted.

After Bill's success as a defense counsel, the base legal officer moved him to the prosecution side. There was always a non-lawyer on the other side so it was not an unequal battle.

The record made at all trials in which non-lawyers participated as counsel was reviewed by the base legal staff. One day Bill was summoned by a real military lawyer who chastened Bill for asking leading questions during the prosecution of a Marine. Bill denied any knowledge of what a leading question was. The lawyer spent the afternoon trying to teach Bill how not to ask leading questions. He was not successful. Bill, like most other trial lawyers, never stopped asking leading questions. In fact, he later became quite proficient at it.

In July, 1954, Bill's two years on active duty came to an end. He had been able to save most of his Marine Corps pay because Mary-Lynn's parents were paying for her senior year at OU while she lived at home.

On his way to Oklahoma, Bill boarded a military transport plane in Tokyo, Japan, and found himself in a seat next to a full colonel. When the man identified himself as John Smith from Oklahoma, Bill remembered seeing a billboard outside Lexington, Oklahoma, proclaiming the town as home of Major John L. Smith, first Marine ace of World War II. Sure enough, Bill's new friend was that military hero.[8]

The transport made a refueling stop at Midway Island where Bill had a chance to look around the island that he found fascinating because of the Battle of Midway, the turning point of World War II in the Pacific. Bill was intrigued with the gooney birds that ran wild on the island. The feathered friends were reputed to be a stupid bird as they wandered on and off runways and otherwise seemed unaware of their surroundings or circumstances.

The remainder of the flight home was normal except for the fact that the co-pilot announced on the leg from Hawaii to San Francisco that one of the four engines on the transport had failed. The aviator said the aircraft could easily make it to Travis Air Force Base on three engines, although Bill worried a little about that promise. The flight was diverted to land at the North Island Naval Air Station in Coronado, California. Bill thoroughly enjoyed the next two days of enjoying the paradise setting of Coronado. He liked it so much that he later bought a condominium there.

Bill's final days on active duty were spent at Treasure Island, a military facility in San Francisco Bay. It took about a week to process his departure from the Marine Corps. After a short session of paperwork each day, Bill caught a city bus and crossed the Oakland Bay Bridge into San Francisco. He spent a lot of time seeing the sights and visiting other Marines at the Marine Memorial Club, a hotel, restaurant, and bar operated as a non-profit venture by Marines.[9]

From San Francisco, Bill flew to Oklahoma City and arrived in the Sooner State on a hot July day. In fact, when Bill was reunited with Mary-Lynn in Norman and was watching the nightly news, the weatherman said Pauls Valley, at 113 degrees, had been the hottest spot in the nation that day. After a couple of days in Norman at his in-laws' home, Bill returned to the family farm in Pauls Valley to take his place in the dairy operation.[10]

Bill's return was timely. His brother, Homer, Jr., had graduated from OU, was also the student battalion commander of the NROTC unit, and left for basic Marine training at Quantico two days after Bill returned. After training, Homer, Jr. was assigned to an anti-aircraft battery and served in Japan and South Korea.[11]

One of Bill's fondest Marine Corps memories occurred when he was president of the American Bar Association (ABA). General E. E. Anderson, a retired Marine four-star general, was active in the ABA and invited Bill to visit with General James L. Jones, Commandant of the Marine Corps. It was not just a visit, but a special invitation to be the guest of honor at the famed Marine Sunset Parade at the Marine Corps facility in Washington, D.C. It was where the Marine Corps Band, "the President's own," and the Marine Corps Drum and Bugle Corps, "the Commandant's own," were stationed.

Bill and several of his Marine Corps friends from Oklahoma attended the ceremony. First there was a reception in the John Phillip Sousa Music Hall where the Marine Corps Band practices. Bill, as the guest of honor, made some remarks. Then the guests adjourned to the reviewing stands where, at dusk, they were treated to an inspiring performance by a Marine Precision Drill Team dressed in blue jackets and white trousers, the summer uniform.[12]

During a stirring performance of the Marine Corps
Drum and Bugle Corps, trumpets blared from atop a building
overlooking the drill field. At the appointed time, Bill was
called forward to stand by General Terrence Dake, the
Assistant Commandant of the Marine Corps, as the Marines
marched past in review. For Bill, it was "a thrilling occasion."

Always proud of his Marine service, Bill held an American Bar Association Board
of Governors meeting in San Diego, California, in 1999. He wanted the lawyers to
experience a military "dining in." Left to right, Bill's wife, Barbara, Bill, and Major
General Henry P. Osman, commander of the United States Marine Corps Recruit
Depot in San Diego. *Courtesy Bill and Barbara Paul.*

Bill and Barbara were guests in the quarters of General Terence Dake, Assistant Commandant of the Marine Corps. *Courtesy Bill and Barbara Paul.*

After the parade, and refreshments at the Assistant Commandant's residence, the entourage gathered at The Crow's Nest, a nice bar in the Willard Hotel. The former Marines each related a memorable event about his service in the Corps. Bill will never forget the story told by General Anderson. As a second lieutenant, Anderson served on the USS Yorktown during the Battle of Midway in World War II. Although the United States Navy achieved a great victory in the battle, Anderson's ship was sunk. General Anderson described the tension-filled hours after he was blown into the water by the explosion that sunk the ship. He and fellow crew members were rescued by a Navy destroyer, ironically named the USS Anderson.

RETURN TO LAW SCHOOL

When I returned to law school, I was determined to maintain
the record of superior academic performance which I had
in my undergraduate years.
— Bill Paul

After six weeks on the farm, Bill rented an apartment
in a university-owned housing complex known as Pace
Apartments. The complex was southeast of the campus, but
not close enough to walk to class. The Pauls' friends, Lee
and Mary Ann West, were arriving 30 days later after Lee's
discharge from the Marines, so Bill rented them an apartment
across the hall. Below the Pauls was Sam Daniel, Jr., a
freshman law student who had returned from active duty in
the Air Force.[1]

Bill's financial condition was rotten during his first year
of law school. Their car was eight years old and unreliable.
They were saving the $2,500 Bill had saved in Korea for a
down payment on a home after law school. Mary-Lynn had

not completed her degree work. Her parents had paid for the first four years—but a fifth year of classes had to be paid for by Bill. The only family income was a small monthly allowance from the farm and $135 a month from the GI Bill.[2]

Bill returned to law school determined to do well academically. Other than for weekend trips to the farm to help his mother, he had no serious diversions and "hit the books." When the grades were released at the end of the first semester of what was his junior year, he had an A or A+ in every class and was ranked first in his class. That first semester after his return was the only time Bill ranked first in his class. In the next three semesters that honor went to Lewis Mosburg. Bill

The freshman class of the OU School of Law in 1951. Bill is third from the left on the front row. To the right of him are future United States Senator Fred Harris and United States District Judge Lee West. The officers of the class were future celebrities. They included West as president, Harris as vice president, future Oklahoma Attorney General G.T. Blankenship as treasurer, and Bill as Honor Council representative. *Courtesy Bill and Barbara Paul.*

became friends with another academic leader in the class, Don Winn of Amarillo, Texas.

Bill and Lee West studied together and became teammates in the annual moot court competition in the spring semester of their junior year. It was an appellate exercise in which students wrote and submitted a brief, a reply brief, and made an oral argument. The top two teams participated in oral argument on Law Day at the College of Law before justices of the Oklahoma Supreme Court.

Bill and West made the finals and won the $100 prize given by the Oklahoma City law firm of Embry, Crowe, Tolbert, Boxley, and Johnson, the firm that Bill would later join. Forty dollars of the prize was given to the other team that made the finals, so Bill and West took home $30 each—a sum greatly appreciated in tight-budget times.[3]

At the end of the junior year, Bill was selected to be on the Board of Editors of the *Oklahoma Law Review*, a prestigious honor for law students. Don Winn was editor-in-chief.

Bill and West also revisited rodeo activity. Their classmate, later Oklahoma Lieutenant Governor and State Treasurer Leo Winters, promoted and produced a student rodeo.

Bill and West entered the wild cow-milking contest. West, a native of Antlers, in southeast Oklahoma, was a fair cowboy with roping experience. His job was to rope the cow. Because Bill had experience with cows on the dairy farm, his job was to milk the animal. West was 50 percent accurate by lassoing one horn of the wild cow that easily escaped. Bill remembered, "Frankly, I was relieved. The cows I had been milking were tame—this one was not!" [4]

Later, Homer, Jr. returned from active duty in the Marines and entered a wild mule-riding contest with fellow law student "Cowboy" Dwight Griggs. They caught their mule and won the event. The next issue of the law school student newspaper contained a headline, "Law Students Best Wild Ass." Thereafter, the publication was censored by law school administrators. [5]

The summer before Bill's final year in law school was active. He worked as much as he could on the farm. He often took Lee West with him to Pauls Valley. West became close to Bill's mother and was one of her biggest fans. West said, "Helen was one of the most wonderful and beautiful women I ever met. She bonded immediately with people of diverse backgrounds. She could find a kindred spirit in almost everybody." [6]

An exciting adventure for Bill was a trip to Madison, Wisconsin, to buy a trailer load of Holstein heifers. West had introduced Bill to cattleman Jack Cornelius of Antlers who gave Bill the benefit of his experience. At the time, there was very little prime dairy stock in Oklahoma and Bill wanted to upgrade the family farm's herd with Holstein cows that could produce nine to ten gallons of milk per day.

A cattle buyer served as Bill's agent as they traveled from farm to farm looking over bred heifers. They made offers on cattle they liked. Bill also got to know several Wisconsin farmers who were self-reliant and militantly independent. When Bill's agent offered one young farmer a certain price for two heifers, the farmer said, "No! I won't sell them to you for that. I'd rather send them to Oscar Mayer than to take that price." Bill met the farmer's price and bought the heifers, part of the 17 head he bought in Wisconsin and transported to the farm in Pauls Valley.

The Holsteins made an appreciable difference in milk production. Based upon past production of Jersey cows, each of the new Holsteins became a "veritable milk factory." [7]

Bill also served as a summer intern in the law office of T.R. Benedum, a prominent Norman attorney. Between working in the law office and on the farm, he sandwiched two weeks of active duty training at the School of Naval Justice at Newport, Rhode Island.

The highlight of his summer legal work was assisting his uncle, Haskell Paul, in a jury trial in Pauls Valley. With the permission of the trial judge, Joe Shumate, Bill gave part of the closing argument. It was a land condemnation case in which the City of Pauls Valley was taking property from a landowner for use as a municipal lake. The jury gave Haskell Paul's client a good recovery. Bill was generously paid $500 for his part in the trial.[8]

Bill's final year in law school was much easier financially. Mary-Lynn was an elementary school teacher in Norman and Earl Sneed, dean of the law school, gave Bill a job as a part-time research assistant. With the two new sources of income and with only Bill attending classes, the financial situation was manageable.

But at the same time, very serious problems arose in Bill and Mary-Lynn's marriage. It was an extremely unhappy year for both of them, but they stayed together for seven more years and had two children. In 1962 they separated and were divorced a few months later.

The last two years of law school were very rewarding for Bill from a professional point of view. He finished near the top of his class, was elected to the Order of the Coif—the Phi Beta Kappa equivalent for the law school—and felt well prepared for a career in the practice of law.

It was decision time for Bill—where would he practice law? Many of his friends had taken positions in Oklahoma City or Tulsa. However, Bill's objective was to practice law in a mid-sized community—smaller than Oklahoma City or Tulsa—but larger than his hometown of Pauls Valley.

Norman fit that description so Bill talked with T.R. Benedum for whom he had interned the previous summer. Benedum offered Bill a position that might lead to a partnership in three or four years.

Another option for Bill was to become a law clerk for Alfred P. Murrah, chief judge of the United States Court of Appeals for the Tenth Circuit. Murrah was a legendary judge whose primary office was in Oklahoma City. Bill had great respect for Murrah and knew what a great opportunity a clerkship for the judge would be. But in his innermost thoughts, he wanted to practice law. Bill traveled to Oklahoma City and met with Judge Murrah who understood Bill's feelings. Murrah said, "I know how you feel. So go ahead and get your feet wet." [9]

Bill talked his options over with several of his friends and decided to take Benedum's offer. He was eager to get started in his practice and begin using all the knowledge he had gained in law school to help clients. Benedum had a good general practice, was very successful, and was a hard worker.

Bill reported for work in his nicest suit, anxious to begin seeing clients and sporting his new law license at the Cleveland County courthouse.

Bill is at left on the seventh row of his senior law school class in 1956. *Courtesy Bill and Barbara Paul.*

Bill when he began the practice of law in 1957 at the Embry-Crowe firm in
Oklahoma City. Courtesy Bill and Barbara Paul.

FLEDGLING LAWYER

"Willie" doesn't sound very professional.
I was wondering if we could call you "Bill."
—Raymond Tolbert

Bill began practice with T.R. Benedum in Norman with high hopes. However, even though Bill was learning about office and courtroom procedure, Benedum did not delegate work to him or make use of his skills. Benedum had a highly-personalized practice and gave Bill only menial tasks to complete. Bill could see that he was not on a good career track.[1]

What made matters worse was Bill's frequent visits with his law school friends who were enjoying their jobs in the major metropolitan areas of the state and talked about bright futures with progressive law firms. In February, 1957, Bill "talked things through" with Benedum and told him he needed to make a change. Benedum was very supportive and told Bill he hoped after he got some experience elsewhere, perhaps he would return to his office. Bill was thankful that the parting was amicable.[2]

Bill began looking for an association in Oklahoma City. He sought advice from Dean Earl Sneed who first mentioned the firm of Embry, Crowe, Tolbert, Boxley, & Johnson (Embry-Crowe). Sneed said the firm always was looking for outstanding young lawyers. Bill was flattered that Sneed thought he might fit that description. Sneed said he would be glad to contact Raymond Tolbert, a senior partner of the firm who was in charge of recruiting new lawyers.[3]

Bill began seeking information about Embry-Crowe. With 16 attorneys, it was the largest law firm in Oklahoma. The firm began in 1902 when Charles Edward "Oley" Johnson opened the first law office in Oklahoma Territory on West Grand Avenue, now Sheridan Avenue, in downtown Oklahoma City.[4]

Johnson, an emigrant from Sweden who graduated from law school at the University of Texas, formed the territory's first law partnership the following year when he joined forces with Albert P. Crockett. In 1905, the firm moved into Oklahoma City's first skyscraper, the six-story Lee Building at the northeast corner of Main Street and Robinson Avenue.[5]

John Embry, a former United States Attorney for Oklahoma Territory, joined the firm in 1916. Vincil Penny "V.P." Crowe became a partner in 1929. Crowe, a graduate of the University of Missouri and former Oklahoma assistant attorney general, became a principal in the firm after a few years.[6]

By the time Bill interviewed in 1957, the firm was called Embry, Crowe, Tolbert, Boxley, & Johnson. Oley Johnson's name had been dropped because of his death in 1950 and the name of Bruce H. Johnson had been added. The two Johnsons were not related. Embry was still living, but no longer active. Crowe was considered one of the state's great lawyers.[7]

There were other reasons that Bill considered working for Embry-Crowe. One of the associates in the firm was William J. Holloway, Jr., with whom Bill had been friends since college days at OU. Holloway, later a distinguished judge on the United States Court of Appeals for the Tenth Circuit, was the son of an Oklahoma governor. The younger Holloway graduated from Harvard Law School, worked in the Department of Justice in Washington, D.C., and had returned to Oklahoma City to practice law. Also, one of Bill's college debate partners, James A. Peabody, was the most recently hired associate at the firm.[8]

Bill explored another possibility—the growing and expanding Kerr-McGee Corporation. While working for T.R. Benedum in Norman, Bill had worked on a matter involving Kerr-McGee and had become acquainted with F.C. Love, then executive vice president of the company. Love had been a partner in the Embry-Crowe firm and learned of Bill's desire to practice law in Oklahoma City.

At that time, Kerr-McGee had only one staff lawyer and was considering hiring another. Love said that, as had been his experience, there might be an opportunity later to move from the legal department to management at Kerr-McGee. It was a pleasant interview in which Bill shared his feelings of preferring the private practice of law in a firm. Even though Love understood, and certainly recommended his old firm, he offered the legal department job to Bill who was grateful for

Love's confidence in his potential.[9]

Bill had to meet with all senior partners at Embry-Crowe. He worked hard on presenting his resume to include his experience and academic achievement. V.P. Crowe told Bill his was the best record he had ever seen. Raymond A. Tolbert, the firm's managing partner and OU Law School graduate, spent a great deal of time with Bill and provided an interview he will never forget.[10]

Tolbert was a distinguished lawyer who had no children and whose vision was to build the firm. Bill remembered, "The quality of his character was communicated to me by just being in the same room with him. He knew what kind of law firm he wanted. In a sense, he was the principal keeper of the values of the firm and he instilled those values into the people he hired." [11]

Mr. Crowe offered Bill a position as an associate with Embry-Crowe. He asked Bill what salary he thought he should command. When Bill asked for $400 a month, Crowe gave him $425. To Bill, it was a huge raise.

With his enormous new monthly salary, Bill looked forward to days when he might be able to buy a suit that was not on sale and purchasing a new car. To that point in his life, he had owned only used cars. For the first few months after going to work for Embry-Crowe, Bill rode a bicycle to the bus station in Norman and commuted between Oklahoma City and Norman by bus.[12]

Mr. Tolbert ran the law firm with strict discipline. His ethical and moral standards were the highest and he served the Oklahoma Bar Association by lecturing around the state on law office management practices which could improve the efficiency and economics of a law office. Each day he opened the firm's mail, reviewed it, and distributed it to the lawyer involved.

That hands-on approach to management led to an embarrassing incident a few weeks after Bill began work at Embry-Crowe in March, 1957. Bill had been wagering on football "parlay cards" in partnership with a clerk at the county courthouse in Norman. One weekend they won, and Bill's partner mailed him $20 in cash. When the money arrived at the office, Tolbert saw it and sent Bill one of his famous notes simply signed with a large red "T." The note said, "Mr. Paul, please arrange to have this kind of mail sent to your home." [13]

Tolbert's strict standards were a subject of office conversation among young associates. Bill quickly heard the story of a junior lawyer who came close to real trouble when he spilled liquor in his office. It was tradition for the firm to be open on Saturday morning and the associate had a flask of liquor that he was taking to the OU football game that afternoon.

After the spill, the smell of liquor permeated the law offices and Tolbert paced the halls trying to discover the source. Tolbert did not drink alcohol and, out of respect, no one drank in his presence. The junior lawyer, in a high state of fear and fright, removed his trousers and used his under shorts as a mop to remove the offending liquid.[14]

During Bill's first week of employment, he was summoned to Mr. Tolbert's office to talk about his name. Bill

was known as "Willie" to almost everyone. Mr. Tolbert began
the conversation with a story of partner John Swinford who
had come to the firm as "Johnny." Mr. Tolbert said "Johnny"
was not a professional name and Swinford became "John."

Then Mr. Tolbert said, "You know, Willie does not sound
very professional either and I was wondering if we could
have your approval to call you 'Bill.'" Although Bill liked
his nickname, and still does, he was not so attached to it as to
create a problem with his new employer. Bill told Mr. Tolbert,
"You are paying my salary, so you can certainly call me Bill."
So that day, Willie Paul became Bill Paul. Everyone in the
firm, including Bill's old friends, Bill Holloway and James
Peabody, began calling him Bill. Today, old friends still call
him Willie—people who have met him since 1957 call him
Bill.[15]

Bill was fortunate to gain experience in several
substantive areas of the law under the tutelage of the firm's
senior specialists in the field. As the firm moved into new
offices in a new addition to the First National Building at
120 Park Avenue, Bill began working on cases that gave him
a unique perspective on areas of state and federal law that
would benefit him as he rose in importance in the firm.

He worked with C. Harold Thweatt and George Guysi
in examining titles for oil and gas clients and DeWitt Kirk
in probate and trust cases. Fred Dunlevy was his mentor
in real property law, as was John Swinford in banking and
commercial transactions and Bruce H. Johnson in estate and
gift taxation. Bill also worked under the tutelage of Val Miller
and James C. "Jim" Gibbens. But Bill especially enjoyed

working with V.P. Crowe, the chief "litigator" or trial lawyer in the firm. Bill's preference was to spend as much time as he could in the courtroom—he wanted to be a trial lawyer.[16]

During his early years at Embry-Crowe, Bill had the opportunity to work on major litigation cases. Mr. Crowe asked Bill to assist him in a criminal case in which a member of a prominent Oklahoma City family had been charged with assault with a deadly weapon. The defense was that the victim was a trespasser on land owned by the client's family. It was a fascinating experience for Bill to interview witnesses and help Mr. Crowe prepare the case for trial.[17]

"Mr. Crowe was a stern taskmaster," Bill remembered. The first time Bill entered his senior partner's office to summarize his interviews with potential witnesses, Mr. Crowe offered wise words of criticism, "Bill, I'd like to hear less of your impressions and analysis, and more of what the witness saw, what the witness did, and what the witness said." It was a good lesson.[18]

Bill was treated generously by Mr. Crowe who allowed his young lawyer to complete substantially all the work to ready a case for hearing or trial. Even during the trial, Bill was allowed to question some witnesses, argue motions to the judge, and make part of the closing argument. It was training that most young lawyers never enjoyed.

Another big case that Bill was allowed to participate in was an unfair competition action in which Embry-Crowe represented Prudential Insurance Company of America, one of the largest life insurance companies in the nation. The litigation arose after a small Oklahoma company selected the

name "Prudential Life and Casualty Insurance Company."
The huge Prudential objected to the Oklahoma company
using its well-known name for selling insurance.[19]

Prudential officers said the Oklahoma case was the most
important national litigation in which the insurance giant
was involved. They believed that if the law allowed a tiny
Oklahoma company to use its name, it would not be long
until companies in other states could use the name Prudential.
There was no doubt Prudential saw confusion and a dilution
of their company's good name should that occur.

One of Bill's most challenging assignments as a young
lawyer came during discovery in the Prudential case. He was
to accompany Mr. Crowe to take depositions of executive
officers of Prudential at their home office in Newark, New
Jersey. However, when Mr. Crowe developed a scheduling
conflict, Bill had to appear at the depositions alone.[20]

Bill recalled the trip as a "magnificent and heady
experience for a young lawyer." He worked directly with
Prudential's general counsel and deposed senior executive
officers and prepared evidence needed for the trial. In
researching the case, Bill had become familiar with a new
trial technique of using a public recognition survey conducted
by an expert in marketing. The idea, to show the value of a
name of a company, was first met with skepticism because
some thought a survey to be nothing but a compilation of
hearsay statements—normally not admitted because of the
exclusion of hearsay evidence.[21]

However, Mr. Crowe liked the idea and convinced
Prudential to hire the top expert in the field to design a public

recognition survey and testify as an expert witness at the
trial. The results of the survey were compelling. Almost all
members of the public who were interviewed believed that
the small Oklahoma company called Prudential was actually
the big Prudential with the Rock of Gibraltar as its marketing
logo.

Mr. Crowe and Bill lost the first two rounds of the
battle when the Oklahoma Insurance Commissioner and the
Oklahoma County District Court denied Prudential relief. But
the result was different on appeal to the Oklahoma Supreme
Court. The high court ultimately prohibited the small
company from using the Prudential name and established
the right of parties to admit public recognition surveys into
evidence.[22]

During the oral argument in the Prudential case before
the Supreme Court, Bill was allowed to split the one hour
allotted with Mr. Crowe. The veteran lawyer told Bill, "Take
all the time you need and I'll use what's left to conclude
our case." Bill felt deeply about the case and presented an
energetic and fact-filled discussion to the justices. During his
argument, Bill was handed a note from Mr. Crowe that read,
"Bill, you have used 50 minutes of our time!"

Bill quickly wrapped up his presentation. Mr. Crowe
took the balance of the time and, characteristically for him,
presented a brilliant conclusion—although he had only nine
minutes.[23]

The greatest thing that happened to Bill in 1963 was the September 27 wedding to
Barbara Brite at the Crown Heights Methodist Church in Oklahoma City.
Courtesy Bill and Barbara Paul.

ON-THE-JOB TRAINING

*Bill learned quickly under the tutelage of V.P. Crowe. From the
beginning I knew Bill was a special breed.*
—Judge William J. Holloway, Jr.

It was not long until V.P. Crowe showed amazing
confidence in Bill's ability as a lawyer. Bill Holloway, who
had been at the firm since he returned from law school at
Harvard University, saw how Crowe began placing more
responsibility on Bill. Holloway said, "Bill deserved the
immediate confidence shown by Mr. Crowe. Bill was poised
in the courtroom and was a powerful and persuasive
speaker." [1]

Bill's training did not always involve accolades from
Mr. Crowe. Once when Bill wrote a brief in a case in which
he was working with Mr. Crowe, the elder lawyer was
"absolutely brutal" in his criticism. Bill was devastated. He
said, "If my sensitivities had been just a bit more tender, I
would have broken down and cried." [2]

Bill left Mr. Crowe's office crestfallen. He sought solace with Bill Holloway who immediately helped his feelings. Holloway said, "You will feel better if you come into Mr. Crowe's office when he is reviewing one of my briefs and you will see that I fare no better." [3]

Another senior attorney at Embry-Crowe when Bill arrived was Bruce H. Johnson. The Indiana native tax lawyer said Bill had "an agreeable personality," that he worked hard with lots of energy. Johnson, who had practiced law with some of the nation's great tax lawyers in his years with the Bureau of Internal Revenue, thought Bill was "a very able lawyer" and "worked efficiently" with his peers and senior partners at the firm.[4]

One of Bill's most significant early probate cases involved his hometown of Pauls Valley. Some of his closest family friends were T.G. "Bus" and Mary Mays. Mary was Bus' third wife but had been married to the wealthy oil man, banker, and farmer since Bill was six years old. At Bus' funeral in 1958, Mary asked Bill to remain after the service. At a brief discussion, she asked Bill to represent her interests.[5]

It was a great learning experience. Bus had died without a will and had completed no estate planning. In addition to Mary, he left two children and two grandchildren, whose fathers, Bus' sons, preceded him in death. It could have been a legal nightmare. But Bill, with the assistance of Bruce Johnson, guided Mary though substantial issues of federal and state taxes. The estate was closed in about 18 months, a relatively short time for an estate of that size.[6]

Mary, a devout Catholic, was like a godmother to Bill. On the day in 1960 when the final decree was issued in her husband's estate, Mary informed Bill that when Bus died she had prayed that the estate would be settled without controversy. She said her prayers had been answered and that she wanted to show her gratitude by financing the education of a priest. Bill made arrangements with the Oklahoma City diocese for Mary's gift.[7]

During the course of the probate proceedings, Bill made many trips to Pauls Valley and often ended his work day at Mary's home. One stormy night, Mary was concerned about Bill driving back to Oklahoma City and asked him to spend the night. When Bill declined, Mary gave him a St. Patrick's medallion that had been blessed by the Pope. Bill promptly affixed the medallion to the roof of his Volkswagen Beetle.

One morning when Bill was driving a young lawyer, Henry P. Rheinberger, to work at Embry-Crowe, they were slipping and sliding all over the icy highway. The St. Patrick's medallion was jarred from its place on the roof of Bill's car and fell into the front seat. Bill said to Rheinberger, "That's a St. Patrick's medallion and it has been blessed by the Pope." Rheinberger, a Catholic, replied, "Yes, I can see that it is. I also see that St. Patrick wants out!" [8]

Even though much of his time was spent building his law practice, Bill still was active as an officer in the United States Marine Corps Reserve. After he was admitted to the bar, the Marine Corps assigned him a new specialty as a legal officer. Because the Marines did not have a separate group of legal officers, it became necessary for Bill to undergo annual training as both a line officer and legal officer.

Summer training involved two-week assignments at the
Amphibious Warfare School in Coronado, California, Camp
Pendleton, California, and Quantico, Virginia. Bill also was a
student at the National War College in Washington, D.C. He
received Marine legal training at Newport, Rhode Island and
San Diego, California. At the Marine Corps Recruit Depot
he reviewed records of courts martial, prepared wills for
Marines going overseas, and counseled unit commanders on
the provisions of the Uniform Code of Military Justice. Bill
was active in the Marine Corps Reserve until 1975, with a
retirement rank of Colonel.[9]

During Bill's first decade, his law firm's name evolved
as partners changed. In 1961, after the deaths of John Embry
and Raymond Tolbert, the firm was known as Crowe, Boxley,
Dunlevy, Thweatt, Swinford, and Johnson. In 1968, after the
death of Calvin Boxley, the firm became Crowe, Dunlevy,
Thweatt, Swinford, Johnson, and Burdick, to include Ben
Burdick who had joined the firm in 1947.

Ultimately, there was a move to institutionalize the name
of the firm which became Crowe & Dunlevy, the largest law
firm in Oklahoma. Mr. Crowe was active from 1929 until his
death in 1974. Dunlevy, who joined the firm in 1937, was
active until his death in 1994.

When Raymond Tolbert, the longtime recruiter for the
firm, died in 1961, the recruiting function of the firm faltered.
Luring new lawyers into the firm was no longer a high
priority. Bill felt an obligation to continue Tolbert's vision of
building the law firm for the future, to make it an institution.

He remembered when Tolbert had stopped by his office after one stormy partners' meeting to say, "The future of this law firm depends upon you and Bill Holloway." [10]

Bill volunteered to assume the firm recruiting role in 1962. He developed a summer intern program, which often resulted in interns being offered jobs as associates in the firm.

Bill also recruited native Oklahomans at regional and national law schools. He looked at the top academic performers in each of the schools and tried to sell students on the benefits of coming to Crowe & Dunlevy. Bill's recruiting class of 1963 was stellar. Andrew "Andy" Coats, later mayor of Oklahoma City and current dean of the OU College of Law, was hired from OU. Allen D. Evans, later one of the premier lawyers in estates and trusts, was hired out of the University of Michigan. James L. Hall, Jr., was hired from Harvard University and became an outstanding health care lawyer. Hall, now deceased, became president of the principal national professional organization for lawyers practicing in the health care field. One of Hall's major clients was Baptist Medical Center, now Integris Baptist Medical Center. [11]

An exciting chapter in Bill's litigation experience involved an anti-trust lawsuit that the State of Oklahoma filed against all major corporations that produced and sold liquid asphalt in the state. Among the defendants were Phillips Petroleum Company, Kerr-McGee Corporation, and Apco Oil Corporation. Attorney General Charles Nesbitt accused the companies of fixing the prices of asphalt which the state paid for highway construction projects. [12]

Assistant Attorney General Burck Bailey managed

the case for the State of Oklahoma. Mr. Crowe was hired by Apco and asked Bill to assist him. Coleman Hayes of Oklahoma City represented Kerr-McGee. Tulsa attorneys Truman Rucker, James Eagleton, and Richard McDermott represented other defendants.

The asphalt price-fixing case was complicated and required many depositions and other forms of discovery. Thousands of documents had to be reviewed. In most instances, the state had directly purchased asphalt from the defendants. On other occasions, the state claimed to have been an indirect purchaser from a middle-man, a contractor that performed highway construction for the State Highway Department.

It was in the second class of transactions in which Bill spent much of his time. He was given the task of gathering facts and evidence to defend the state's claim. A few weeks before the case was set for trial, Mr. Crowe broke his neck during a fall down a staircase in his home. Because Mr. Crowe was such a key player on the defense team, the defendants asked for a continuance.[13]

However, Assistant Attorney General Bailey "played a master card." He dismissed Crowe & Dunlevy's client, Apco, from the case and told the judge he wanted the trial to be heard as scheduled. Bailey could make such a move because if he could prove there was a price-fixing conspiracy, each of the defendants would be separately liable. It would not be a financial loss for the State of Oklahoma even if Apco did not actively participate in the trial. The judge agreed with Bailey and refused to grant a continuance.

Because Crowe & Dunlevy had so much time invested in the case, it was decided that Bill should join the Kerr-McGee defense team headed by Coleman Hayes. Bill still reported daily to Mr. Crowe, first at the hospital, then at home. Bill said, "For him, it was like being a great racehorse locked in his stall watching other horses run a race. He could hardly stand it, but he had a serious injury and had no choice but to stay in a hard cast for several weeks." [14]

The facts of the asphalt price-fixing case were not good for the defendants and Bailey made the most of it. During the long trial that established Bailey as an outstanding young trial lawyer, witness after witness came forth to help prove the State's case that the oil companies had conspired to charge an inflated price for asphalt. One day when the case had gone particularly well for the State, a representative of Phillips Petroleum Company who had been attending the trial said, "For sometime I have been thinking that this case would never end—but now I am afraid it will!" His premonition was correct.[15]

The jury found the defendants guilty of fixing the prices of liquid asphalt and rendered a huge verdict in favor of the State of Oklahoma. However, on the second tier of the litigation, the jury found there was no conspiracy to fix prices and no violation of law in instances when the asphalt was sold to highway contractors. That was the area of the litigation in which Bill had spent so much time. Even though the defendants were greatly affected by the outcome of the lawsuit, Bill was satisfied with the results in the indirect purchase claims in which he had gathered and prepared the evidence.[16]

The federal court trial in the liquid asphalt case was just the beginning of the litigation. Eventually, the defendants that took part in the trial settled while the case was on appeal and requested Apco contribute to the settlement. However, the applicable law did not require Apco to pay any of the judgment rendered against the other companies that remained in the lawsuit and Apco refused to do so.

Apco's problems were far from over. When Mr. Crowe died in 1974 Bill became lead counsel for the oil company that became a defendant in a class action lawsuit filed by counties in Oklahoma alleging they had been victims of the asphalt price-fixing conspiracy. Clyde Muchmore assisted Bill in preparation of Apco's defense. The class action lawsuit filed by the counties was settled before trial.[17]

Bill and his litigation team won a complete victory for Apco in the final chapter of the asphalt price-fixing saga. Because Apco did not pay any part of the federal court judgment, the State of Oklahoma decided to pursue Apco under the state anti-trust statutes in state court. With help from Muchmore and John J. Griffin, Jr., a new associate in the firm, Bill argued that Apco should prevail as a matter of law because the State of Oklahoma was not a "person" who was given the right under state law to bring an anti-trust action. The Supreme Court of Oklahoma agreed with Apco's position and the company was relieved of any duty to pay damages to the State. The ten-year battle over asphalt price-fixing finally came to an end.[18]

Bill's litigation experience included eminent domain

cases in which the State of Oklahoma or some other government entity took private property for a public purpose. Bill represented many landowners in Garvin County whose land was being taken for construction of Interstate Highway 35. The trials were held in Bill's hometown of Pauls Valley.

Bill also handled two major will contests. One case involved the estate of Charles Morton Share, one of the most significant cases ever in Woods County, Oklahoma. He gained valuable experience in a major bankruptcy proceeding in Oklahoma City that involved several apartment complex developments, representing Metropolitan Life Insurance Company, and the Liberty National Bank and Trust Company of Oklahoma City.[19]

One of the pitfalls of being on the defense side of litigation was in representing insurance companies as named defendants. Bill discovered the prejudice that some juries had against "big" insurance companies when he represented the Prudential Insurance Company in a disability policy claim in state court in McAlester, Oklahoma. He knew it was not a good sign when the judge admonished the jury at the end of the trial, "Now don't be too long in your deliberations. Keep in mind that this is the first day of deer season." The jury obeyed the judge and returned a verdict for the plaintiff 30 minutes later.[20]

Family law was an area of practice in which Bill spent a significant amount of time. He handled a number of high-profile divorce cases. In one case he represented Mary Wilkinson in the divorce case against her husband, Bud Wilkinson, the revered former OU football coach. Mary hired

Bill on the recommendation of his law school dean, Earl
Sneed, who was a senior executive of Liberty National Bank,
one of Crowe & Dunlevy's principal clients. Fortunately,
the divorce case was settled without trial. Bill was assisted
by Andy Coats. Coach Wilkinson was ably represented by
Dick Taft, a co-founder of the McAfee & Taft law firm in
Oklahoma City.[21]

    Bill learned the value of settling a case—rather than
going to trial—from a comment made by one of his clients,
Alfred A. Drummond, a Marshall County rancher who
happened to be in Bill's office one day when he was preparing
for trial in another matter. Drummond said, "On any day of
the week, a bad settlement is better than a very good
lawsuit." [22]

BUILDING AN INSTITUTION

Bill saw far into the future and realized that Crowe & Dunlevy would maintain its leadership and stability only if major changes were brought about. Had Bill not been in control, there may not have been a Crowe & Dunlevy today.
—Judge William J. Holloway, Jr.

During his first 15 years at Crowe & Dunlevy, Bill received vast experience in both courtroom litigation and in a variety of non-trial areas of the law. Andy Coats said, "Bill could do more things in the law and do them better than anyone. He is the most able, competent, and hardest working lawyer I have known." [1]

One area which he pioneered was bank charter litigation. In the 1940s and 1950s, very few new state banks were chartered by the Oklahoma Banking Commission and only a handful of national banks were approved by the Comptroller of the Currency. However, as the state's economy grew in the 1960s, the situation changed and Bill was at the forefront of the change.

He began representing only applicants for new bank charters, although later he represented existing banks that opposed charters for new institutions. Two of Bill's first cases involved establishment of a fourth bank in Norman and the first bank in Mustang, Oklahoma.[2]

A new state bank charter's first test was a hearing before the Oklahoma State Banking Board, chaired by the Banking Commissioner. That was followed by judicial review in a special court, the Court of Bank Review, that had been especially created by the Oklahoma legislature. The special court was composed of three state district court judges. The special court decision could be appealed to the Oklahoma Supreme Court.

Because of the economic significance of the entry of a new bank into a market, almost every application went all the way to the Supreme Court. At one point, Bill won 20 cases in a row, an enviable record in bank charter litigation or any other type of law practice. He invited young associate Andy Coats to participate in many of the bank charter cases.

It was necessary to use expert witnesses such as economists or accountants in the bank charter application process. Bill developed a long-standing relationship with Oklahoma City certified public accountant W. Bryan Arnn. Bill remembered, "He was phenomenal, probably the best expert witness I have ever known." Arnn's credibility was very high, making it easier for Bill to convince the Banking Board and appellate courts that his clients should be given the right to operate a bank in Oklahoma.[3]

Bill developed a great interest in commercial banking and banking law, becoming what Andy Coats described as "the premier bank lawyer in Oklahoma."[4] Crowe & Dunlevy had for some time represented Liberty National Bank and Trust Company of Oklahoma City (Liberty), one of the two major banks in the capital city and among the top four banks in Oklahoma. In the late 1960s, J.W. "Bill" McLean was recruited home to Oklahoma from San Francisco, California, where he worked for the Bank of America. McLean became president and chief executive officer of Liberty.[5]

Shortly after McLean arrived at his new post, he called V.P. Crowe and requested a young lawyer in the firm be assigned to a major project for the bank. Bill was tabbed and reported to McLean. From that beginning, Bill became close to the bank president. When John Swinford left the Liberty board of directors, Bill was invited to take his place. Bill served on the Liberty board for more than 20 years. Later, as Liberty was merged with other institutions, Bill served on the boards of the First National Bank of Tulsa, the Banks of Mid-America, and Bank One.[6]

In the late 1960s, Bill and Mr. Crowe represented Liberty in opposing the creation of a bank holding company by Liberty's principal competitor, First National Bank of Oklahoma City. Liberty lost the battle before federal banking authorities and took its cause to the state legislature. Bill drafted the legislation that was intended to make bank holding companies unlawful. Bill lobbied for passage of the bill which was overwhelmingly approved by both houses of the Oklahoma legislature and signed into law.[7]

The saga of bank holding companies took an ironic twist two years later when Harvey Everest, McLean's predecessor as head of Liberty, called Bill and asked him to perform the legal work to enable Liberty to purchase several smaller banks in Oklahoma City. Bill told Everest that such an action would be a violation of the law sponsored by Liberty. There was no way around the law. However, a few years later, Liberty joined other banks and successfully requested the legislature to repeal the law Bill had written. Bank holding companies have been allowed in Oklahoma since that time.[8]

The personnel of Liberty and the law firm had a close relationship. There was an annual golf and tennis tournament between the two groups, usually followed by an outdoor dinner event at the country home of B.D. Eddie. Some of the more talented members of each organization would put on a hilarious program after dinner, with a lot of laughs, usually at the expense of several of those present.

Included among those at Liberty, or at a successor bank, with whom Bill worked were Morrison Tucker, Willard Boggs, Bob Blinn, Harvey Hinkle, Dewey Jernigan, Orvis Rundle, John Browne, Grady Harris, Vernon Wright, Gerry Marshall, Gordon Greer, Jack White, Bill Bell, Ken Bonds, Joe Semrod, Jim Jennings, Pete Dowling, Jim Bruce, Fred Moses, Mischa Gorkuska, Charles Nelson, Ken Brown, Lou Trost, John Shelley, and Willis Wheat.

Board members with whom Bill served included John Kirkpatrick, John Nichols, Walter Duncan, Guy Anthony, B.D. Eddie, Ray Hefner, Henry Browne, Jr., Dan Hogan, Bob Torray, and Luke Sewell. In Tulsa they included Walter Helmerich, Dr. Don Brawner, W.K. "Bill" Warren, Jr., and Henry Zarrow.

One of the firm's most significant cases involving banking law resulted from the failure of Penn Square Bank in 1982. The bank, located in an Oklahoma City shopping center, had become nationally known for making huge high-risk energy loans funded primarily by major banks around the country.

Crowe & Dunlevy became involved in the Penn Square litigation when Bill received a telephone call on Friday afternoon, July 2, 1982, from the general counsel of Continental Illinois Bank of Chicago, one of the large banks entangled in the Penn Square situation. The bank wanted to immediately engage the services of Crowe & Dunlevy. Bill was hesitant because of the firm's policy of being careful about accepting the first offer of employment in big matters so as to not miss the opportunity to represent a client with major involvement.

Bill asked the Continental Illinois general counsel to what extent his bank was involved. The lawyer responded, "Let me put it this way. Our exposure is in excess of the capital of our bank and our board of directors is at this moment in emergency session considering the crisis." Bill had heard enough, and said, "You have just employed a law firm." Gary Davis, and later, Kent Myers, handled litigation at Crowe & Dunlevy for Continental Illinois and its successor bank in reorganization for several years.

Bill continues to be involved in banking. Since 2004, he has served on the board of Bank2, a banking institution wholly owned by the Chickasaw Nation. Bill agreed to serve on the board in 2005 as a way to help the Chickasaw Nation accomplish its goal of providing banking services to Native America.[9]

Bill spent much of his time promoting the institutional

qualities of Crowe & Dunlevy. He saw other great law firms falter and fade away because partners were not adding the brightest and best young lawyers to build for the future. Bill knew that growing mobility of young lawyers forced the firm to invest significant time in attracting new associates. No longer was Crowe & Dunlevy competing only with local law firms. Top Oklahoma law school graduates were interviewing with firms in Houston, Dallas, and other large cities in the region.

Bill's work in recruiting top lawyers for Crowe & Dunlevy was a lasting contribution to the strength of the firm. Bill Holloway observed, "Had it not been for Bill caring about the institutionalization of the firm, Crowe & Dunlevy might have joined other firms in riding off into the sunset." [10]

Bill assisted legal interns and young lawyers feel their way in their chosen profession. "So many times when I was lost," Andy Coats remembered, "Willie put me on the right track. He got my first client for me and helped me send out my first statement for services rendered. He even gave me his purple, one-speed bicycle to ride to class in my senior year of law school." [11]

After serving as director of recruiting at Crowe & Dunlevy for seven years, Bill believed he was getting older and did not relate to law students as well as he once did. He turned over the recruiting chores to Jim Hall. Bill's last recruit was Clyde Muchmore who joined the firm in 1968 and became one of the premier appellate law practitioners in Oklahoma. Muchmore and Harvey Ellis of Crowe & Dunlevy later wrote the definitive treatise on Oklahoma appellate practice.

When Bill became managing partner of the firm after
the death of V.P. Crowe in 1974, he used his powers of
persuasion to make substantive changes to the internal
structure of Crowe & Dunlevy. As a young lawyer, he had
perceived shortcomings of the firm in compensating and
training young lawyers. He instituted an associate training
program that developed into one of the major administrative
areas of the firm.[12]

The most difficult and most important task Bill undertook
in the administration of Crowe & Dunlevy was the reform
of the lawyer compensation system. By the mid-1960s the
firm employed more than 30 lawyers—20 of them were
considered partners. The compensation system was archaic.
It was based upon principles that worked well in small firms,
but failed in larger firms.[13]

The compensation system had two major, disastrous
flaws. The first was that partners had vested ownership
percentages that could not be changed without the partner's
consent. Any change in the distribution of the firm's earnings
had to be based upon partners being willing to "give up" part
of their vested percentage. The second flaw was that lawyers
were compensated solely on seniority. All the lawyers who
had been at the firm for a certain number of years were
compensated equally, without any regard to their relative
contribution to the firm.[14]

V.P. Crowe was the undisputed leader of the firm and
partners normally fell in line with his wishes. Bill recognized
Mr. Crowe's power and began talking to him about the
need for a change in the compensation system. Bill had
a two-pronged plan—the firm should unilaterally and

periodically fix ownership percentages and foster incentive for achievement by recognizing the disparity in contribution by individual members of a given seniority group.

Mr. Crowe was sympathetic to Bill's view but was slow to do anything about it. Finally, after two years, Mr. Crowe sold the partners on the first half of Bill's proposal. Thereafter, ownership percentages could be changed by a majority of the partners each year after due consideration by a compensation committee. It took ten more years for the second principle of recognizing individual income production and performance to be implemented.[15]

The second principle was not adopted by the firm until after Mr. Crowe's death and Bill's ascension as chairman of the firm's executive committee. The antiquated compensation system cost the firm some good lawyers who were dissatisfied with receiving too small a percentage of the money that they were generating. Others, like Bill, stayed with the firm because they simply preferred to practice there.[16]

Senior tax partner Bruce Johnson backed Bill as chairman of the executive committee. Another key player in the reform of the compensation system was F.C. Love who returned to the firm in an "of counsel" arrangement after he retired as president of Kerr-McGee Corporation. A premier law office management consultant from Philadelphia, Pennsylvania, was hired to interview partners and prepare a comprehensive report with recommendations. Previously, the firm had no financial planning. With help of the consultant, a budgeting process was begun and income goals were established. Setting goals gave the firm a spirit of cooperation—everyone was on the same team.

Bill was part of a five-person executive committee. Other members divided responsibility over economics, administration, recruiting, and career development issues. As part of a plan to guarantee mentoring and professional development, each new associate was paired with a partner.

"Firm administration is no race for the short-winded," Bill reflected, "Lawyers by nature are extremely independent and do not react well to the imposition of any sort of authority." Bill found that each partner in a partnership feels that he or she is the sole captain of his or her destiny. However, as Crowe & Dunlevy matured, an institutional mind set took hold and lawyers of the firm began accepting and appreciating the authority of firm leaders.

One of Bill's early battles was to hire a non-lawyer as office manager. In the past, a lawyer, who theoretically knew how to manage the flow of work and information, served as manager. Bill's first attempt was to hire a skilled manager of a local abstract and title company. It failed because the lawyers would not accept his role or cooperate with him. However, the next non-lawyer, an office manager, was more successful as lawyers became accustomed to the idea. Crowe & Dunlevy now has a human resources manager, an information technology group, an accounting group, a benefits program manager, and a non-lawyer chief financial officer.[17]

Another of Bill's projects was to begin the use of "legal assistants," sometimes called "paralegals." In the 1970s, Crowe & Dunlevy was one of the first firms in the state to use legal assistants when the idea was still novel. Today, legal assistants play an important part in the delivery of legal services in both small and large law firms.

In another move to convince young lawyers to stay with
the firm, Bill drafted a retirement program that limited the
amount of firm earnings that would be paid to "of counsel"
lawyers who had retired from the firm at age 67. His plan,
approved by the partners, provided that not more than
ten percent of annual earnings could be paid to all retired
partners. The Philadelphia consultant so liked Bill's idea that
Bill was invited to appear on panels at national conferences to
speak on law office retirement systems.[18]

The compensation plan that Bill created and that was
approved by a slim majority of partners after a long battle
involved consideration of several factors, not just seniority.
The first year the new compensation plan was in operation,
partners voted Bill an increase in his share, giving him the top
share in the firm. One of Bill's goals, however, was to always
produce more net income than he took from the firm each
year. Because he was involved in representation of significant
clients, and because he worked long hours, he was able to
accomplish that goal every year he was at Crowe & Dunlevy.
Bruce Johnson said, "Bill endeared himself to other partners
because he always brought more money into the firm than
he took out. Others appreciated him making money for them
also." [19]

Bill's leadership of the compensation reform was
founded upon the principle that younger members would
take a lower percentage of their personal production than
the senior members of the firm. This was based upon the
assumption that young lawyers would appreciate the seniors
who had gone before them and built the firm that gave them
their opportunities.

Bill presented a number of ideas to partners. He had dreams and expectations that exceeded the firm's ability to achieve them—but it was exciting to try to implement them. Some of his ideas were rejected by the firm, but many were accepted and successful.

One of Bill's aspirations was to establish a bond practice in the firm. Two small firms were handling most of the bond practice in Oklahoma City. Bill recruited a young lawyer with expertise in bonds. It was determined that Crowe & Dunlevy's entry into the bond field would be helped if a new statewide trust authority with the power to issue bonds was created. Crowe & Dunlevy drafted and supported legislation to that end. When the legislature created the trust authority, Crowe & Dunlevy ended up doing much of the bond work.[20]

Bill served seven years as chair of the executive committee. He probably could have been reelected but chose to spend more time in his litigation practice. He also thought it wise to establish a precedent that no one lawyer become entrenched in an administrative position in the firm. In fact, it became the practice to limit an executive committee chair to a two-year term. That custom remains at Crowe & Dunlevy today.[21]

Bill's service in firm administration was rewarding because he saw the possibility that Crowe & Dunlevy would continue as a venerable and lasting institution. He felt the burden thrust upon him by V.P. Crowe and Raymond Tolbert to make certain the firm would remain at the top of Oklahoma's legal world.

Another of Bill's goals was to mentor and launch legal careers of the younger lawyers in the firm, just as Mr. Crowe had done for him. Subconsciously, he always was looking for a young lawyer who would work with him on major cases with the same intensity with which he had served Mr. Crowe. Bill's goal was realized in Harry A. Woods, Jr., who was intense, dedicated, and serious in purpose.

Woods, from the tiny town of Monroe, Oklahoma, came with the firm after a tour of duty as a Judge Advocate General (JAG) lawyer in the United States Army. He had been a Root-Tilden scholar at the New York University Law School after attending Oklahoma State University. An oft-quoted story by a member of the Root-Tilden scholar selection committee told of Woods' interview. One member of the committee said, "Harry, you are from a very small town and we worry about how you might get along if you get this scholarship and go to law school in New York City." Harry immediately responded, "Well now, don't you worry about that. I've been to Fort Smith twice and I got along just fine." Woods got the scholarship.[22]

After working with Bill on numerous cases, Woods became one of the premier securities law litigators in Oklahoma.

Another young lawyer Bill mentored was Leonard Court, an Oklahoma State University and Harvard University graduate and veteran of the JAG office in the United States Air Force. Even though they became good friends, there were always football partisanship differences. Bill strongly supported OU and Court was the most avid OSU fan Bill knew.

Court worked with Bill in defending Northwestern Mutual Life Insurance Company in an age discrimination lawsuit. As Mr. Crowe had done with Bill, Court was allowed to heavily participate in the trial, including handling half the witnesses and making part of the closing argument to the jury. After the trial, United States District Judge Ralph Thompson told Bill privately that Court's performance was one of the best he had ever seen from a young lawyer. Court now heads up a large group of lawyers in the firm that specializes in employment law.[23]

Bill saw other terrific lawyers with whom he worked develop their skills at Crowe & Dunlevy. John J. Griffin, Jr., is now a specialist in oil and gas law. Mark Grossman is a well-known litigator and specialist in appellate law. Andy Coats is now dean of the OU School of Law and a past president of the American College of Trial Lawyers. Richard Ford is a distinguished trial lawyer. Marion Bauman became an expert in the banking law field.

Pat Ryan became United States Attorney for the Western District of Oklahoma and participated in the trial and conviction of Timothy McVeigh for the bombing of the Alfred P. Murrah Federal Building in 1995. Arthur F. Hogue has prospered in the practice. Brooke Smith Murphy is a premier litigator, a past president of the Oklahoma County Bar Association, and served as president of Crowe & Dunlevy in 2006-2007.

Included among those who have achieved great distinction in their areas of practice are Robert M. Johnson, Gil Gaddis, Judy Morse, Kent Meyers, Mike Stewart, Jimmy Goodman, Candace Williams, Gary Davis, Jim George, Roger Stong, Mike Laird, Lon Foster, Kenni Merritt, Mark Christiansen, and Molly Tolbert. Molly is married to Miles

Tolbert, Oklahoma Secretary of the Environment, who was with the firm for a short time. Miles' great uncle was Raymond Tolbert, who changed Bill's name from Willie to Bill.[24]

Bill's leadership at Crowe & Dunlevy was not limited to serious subjects such as compensation, retirement, and recruiting. He has always enjoyed a good party and having a good time. While chair of the firm, he started an annual event, a holiday breakfast on the last working day before the Christmas holiday. The event, which is one of the firm's great traditions, comes with entertainment provided by talented amateur performers in the firm.

Bill also started a personal July Fourth celebration in and around his office beginning promptly at 3:30 p.m. on the last working day before the Independence Day holiday. He bought and served champagne. The first year he did not know how many people would attend and he ran out of champagne half way through the celebration. Fortunately, he dispatched a contingent to the Petroleum Club across the street for more champagne. Even after Bill left the firm in 1985, two of his younger partners, Tony Rupert and Mark Grossman, continued to hold the event, dubbed as the "Annual Bill Paul Fourth of July Celebration." The good time is now in its 27th year.[25]

FOUR SEASONS

Arthur Andersen was determined to vigorously defend itself
and its partners.
—Bill Paul

In the early 1970s, Four Seasons Nursing Centers of Oklahoma City attracted the attention of Wall Street. The company's common stock became the second most-active-traded security on the American Stock Exchange. Four Seasons' business was to construct and operate nursing homes for elderly citizens and chronically ill patients.

Trading in the stock was almost irrational. At its high, the stock was selling for more than 70 times the company's earnings. The national accounting firm, Arthur Andersen & Company (Arthur Andersen), based in Chicago, Illinois, but with a large office in Oklahoma City, was Four Seasons' auditor. A few months after the close of the fiscal year and completion of the annual audit, the company experienced serious cash flow difficulties. The three or four years of rapid

(cutline 87) While Bill was involved in some of the state's highest profile legal cases, Barbara was keeping the home fires burning. The Paul family in 1973, left to right, Bill, Barbara, Steve, and Elaine. *Courtesy Bill and Barbara Paul.*

growth had depleted the company's treasury and a federal bankruptcy action was filed.[1]

Arthur Andersen, a client of Crowe & Dunlevy, was named as a defendant in several class action shareholder lawsuits filed against the company and its officers and directors. On the recommendation of Bruce Johnson, the firm's top tax lawyer, Bill was hired as trial counsel for Arthur Andersen. Bill selected Harry A. Woods, Jr., to assist him. What Bill did not know was that the case would have a life of seven years and would become one of the most significant class action securities law cases in the nation.

Bill's early plan was to maintain a low profile in hopes that the focus of the plaintiffs would be on other parties, not Arthur Andersen which served only as the auditor of the company's books. However, it became apparent that Arthur Andersen was the deepest pocket among the defendants—possibly the only defendant that had resources from which to pay a judgment. The result was that Arthur Andersen became the target defendant along with the Wall Street underwriting firm, Walston and Company.

All the class action cases were consolidated into one federal court proceeding that was assigned to United States District Judge Roszel Thomsen, Maryland. Judge Thomsen came to Oklahoma City to preside over a packed courtroom for the first hearing. Not long after the initial hearing, Bill and other counsel received a notice that future hearings would be held in Baltimore, "by agreement of counsel." Bill could find no other lawyer who had consented to moving the hearings half way across the country. However, none of the lawyers wanted to object and upset the newly-assigned judge.

Bill, right, and Homer Paul, left, kiss their mother, Helen Paul, after she was named the Mother of the Year for Oklahoma in 1975. *Courtesy Homer Paul.*

More than a dozen hearings were held in Baltimore over the years. It was a unique experience when the bailiff would enter the courtroom to convene the hearing and announce, "Hear Ye! Hear Ye! Hear Ye! The District Court for the Western District of Oklahoma is now in session!" Observers might have been confused if they walked to the window and saw Baltimore Harbor.[2]

Bill and Woods worked closely in the Four Seasons case with Arthur Andersen's general counsel, Charles Boand, of the Wilson & McIlvane firm of Chicago.

An interesting aspect of the case arose from the State of Ohio being one of the parties. The State Treasurer of Ohio had loaned Four Seasons a lot of money and the company had defaulted on payment of promissory notes. It was a new issue for the federal court as to whether or not the notes were considered "securities" under federal securities law. Judge Thomsen held that they were.

After numerous depositions and production and review of tens of thousands of documents, settlement negotiations began. Charles Boand took the lead for Arthur Andersen in the discussions. Finally a settlement amounting to only a fraction of the claims was reached. Several defendants contributed to the settlement, but Arthur Andersen paid the lion's share.[3]

The settlement did not end the litigation. The State of Ohio waited too long to announce it wanted to opt out of the settlement agreement. However, the State filed a motion contending that it was not bound by the settlement agreement and had the right to pursue its claim individually.

Helen Paul, left, with her son, Homer, and his wife, Ramona, at their wedding. *Courtesy Bill and Barbara Paul.*

Judge Thomsen ruled in favor of Ohio, but the decision was overturned by the United States Court of Appeals for the Tenth Circuit. When the United States Supreme court refused to hear the matter, the decision was final.[4]

There were other parties, however, that did opt out of the settlement in time, reserving the right to go forward on their own. The remaining job for Bill and Woods was to defend those various actions. Settlements were negotiated in all but one of the cases. In that case, a California plaintiff was determined to litigate the matter to the end. There were more hearings, more depositions, and more discovery. The hearings took place in various cities but finally the trial was commenced in San Diego, California, and concluded in Baltimore.

Arthur Andersen was the sole defendant in the trial before Judge Thomsen. At the conclusion of the non-jury trial, the judge ruled in favor of Arthur Andersen. Bill had the great pleasure of calling John Hennessey, the Arthur Andersen partner in charge of litigation, to tell him that Arthur Andersen had succeeded in achieving victory in the only Four Seasons case that had gone to trial.[5]

Bill also was involved in a criminal case involving two Arthur Andersen partners who had worked on the company's audit and were charged with violation of federal securities laws. The principal of Four Seasons had pleaded guilty in a plea bargain arrangement and was sentenced to one year in federal prison.

Arthur Andersen was determined to vigorously defend itself and its partners. The audit firm hired criminal law attorneys from New York City who took the lead in the criminal defense. Bill served in a supporting role in the criminal case in which one of the two Andersen partners was acquitted and as to the other there was a hung jury. Sometime later, the United States Justice Department determined the case would not be retried and the charges against the remaining Arthur Andersen partner were dismissed.[6]

City
OF FAITH

*Reverend Roberts said God spoke to him and told him
to build the hospital.*
— Bill Paul

In 1976, highly successful television evangelist and
university founder, Oral Roberts, determined that his ministry
should construct and operate a major hospital in Tulsa,
Oklahoma. Roberts, a native of Pontotoc County, Oklahoma,
had become the nation's leading television evangelist and
had conducted hundreds of evangelistic and healing crusades
on six continents. In 1963, he established Oral Roberts
University which had a vibrant student body and was
recognized far and wide as an excellent institution of higher
learning.[1]

In his books and magazine Roberts had recounted a
personal experience when he was distraught about a family
tragedy and was wandering in the desert of the southwestern
United States. He said that during the experience, God spoke

to him and told him that he must build a hospital and that God enumerated certain particulars such as that the hospital should be 77 stories high. When Roberts returned to Tulsa, he began to put into motion a plan to carry out what he perceived to be God's instructions.[2]

Under state law in effect at the time, no new hospitals could be built in Oklahoma unless a Certificate of Need (CON) was issued by the Oklahoma Health Planning Commission, made up of the directors of three major state agencies, the Department of Health, the Department of Mental health, and the Department of Human Services. The federal government's mandate was that Medicare, Medicaid, and other federal health assistance programs would be withheld from the state unless the screening for new facilities occurred.[3]

Shortly after lawyers for Roberts filed an application for a CON, Bill received a call from two high profile Tulsa lawyers who happened to be Bill's good friends. The lawyers were Thomas Brett and James Ellison, both of whom later were appointed to the federal district court bench. Brett regularly represented St. Francis Hospital and Ellison was counsel for Hillcrest Hospital in Tulsa. Both hospitals were principal members of the Tulsa Area Hospital Council (TAHC).

At first, Bill was perplexed why such great lawyers as Brett and Ellison wanted him to get involved in the litigation. But he understood when the Tulsa attorneys explained that the application for what would be called City of Faith Hospital was divisive in the Tulsa community and they had recommended that the hospitals opposing the City of Faith application hire counsel from outside the Tulsa area. Bill was flattered that Brett and Ellison had recommended him to handle this unique case which was attracting national interest.[4]

The first thing that Bill did was to form a litigation team at Crowe & Dunlevy. He invited Richard C. "Rick" Ford, a senior associate in the firm, to join the team. Ford was an example of Bill's belief that law firms strive mightily to hire brilliant law students because they will be intellectually superior to the firm's partners. Bill also believed that was the case with Ford, although he never admitted that to him.

Bill also asked Earl Sneed to participate. Sneed had been dean of the University of Oklahoma School of Law when Bill was a student and was a legendary lawyer and bank president. After retiring as president of Liberty National Bank and Trust Company of Oklahoma City, Sneed had joined Crowe & Dunlevy.

Bill thought Sneed was especially qualified to take part in the litigation because he was from the Tulsa area and was highly visible in public affairs. He had led the fight for judicial reform in Oklahoma in the previous decade and had served as mayor of Norman. He also was president-elect of the Oklahoma Bar Association. Tragically, Sneed died in December, 1979, during the City of Faith litigation.[5]

A major issue in the case was whether there was a need for additional hospital beds in the Tulsa area. After all, that was the focus of the federal legislative policy that mandated the state establish a screening agency. The policy was simple—if the need for additional beds could not be shown, a CON should not be issued and the facility would not be built.

The effect of the federal policy was to avoid the needless
investment of resources in any area that had sufficient
healthcare facilities.

A unique aspect of the City of Faith case was the deeply
interwoven relationship between religion and the delivery
of healthcare as envisioned by Oral Roberts Ministries.
Each patient was to have a physician and a prayer partner.
Laying on of hands was deemed to be an important aspect of
healthcare delivery.[6]

In early research for the case, Rick Ford identified an
issue raised by the City of Faith application that appeared
to be in violation of the Establishment Clause of the federal
constitution. That clause requires that all governmental
entities must avoid any sectarian involvement with respect to
any religion. The concept is generally known as separation
of church and state. The particular governmental action
under scrutiny must reflect a clearly secular, or non-sectarian
purpose, must not have the effect of advancing or inhibiting
any religion, and must have avoided excessive governmental
entanglement with religion. Bill reviewed Ford's research and
agreed that this was a serious issue which should be advanced
by TAHC.[7]

Bill's opponents in the City of Faith litigation were
members of a Tulsa law firm, Moyers, Martin, Conway,
Santee and Imel. The most active lawyers in the fight over
the CON were Don Moyers and Bill's law school classmate,
Jack Santee. Santee was also a close friend and former varsity
football player at OU.

The initial activity in the case was at the administrative
level and was very political. The Oklahoma Health

Planning Commission used a citizens' advisory group to hear applications and make non-binding recommendations. Hearings were held and both sides presented evidence. Through his television ministry, Roberts requested letters of support be submitted to the OHPC. More than 400,000 letters were received.

Bill's evidence was that the outstanding Tulsa hospitals were fully staffed by qualified and experienced medical personnel and that each one had empty beds. On average, the occupancy rate at the three large hospitals was 92 percent. Lawyers for Roberts argued that City of Faith would be unique, would draw from a national constituency of patients who had a preference for holistic medicine as would be practiced there, and that the patient bed occupancy of the existing Tulsa hospitals would not be adversely affected.[8]

During the course of the proceedings, the City of Faith applicants did reduce the number of beds for which they sought approval from 777 to 294. However, the issues remained the same. Roberts assembled a talented group of physicians and administrators and both sides stayed away from the issue of whether or not God had spoken to Roberts about building the hospital. Neither set of lawyers mentioned anything about the experience.

However, at one of the hearings, a member of the citizens' advisory group could not refrain from bringing up the alleged conversation with God. After the doctor who was slated to be chief of the medical staff at City of Faith completed his testimony, the chairman of the advisory committee asked if anyone had questions. One member asked, "Doctor, do you really believe that God spoke to Oral

Roberts about this hospital?"

The answer was immediate, possibly because the question may have been anticipated. Bill called it "the most brilliant response I have ever heard in a courtroom." The doctor replied, "Yes, just as surely as he spoke to Moses through the burning bush." [9]

Another humorous event took place outside the hearings. Reverend Roberts had related on television that while he was feeling the burden of the battle for City of Faith, a 900-foot Jesus appeared and lifted the City of Faith complex on his shoulders to lighten Roberts' load. Shortly thereafter, a sign appeared on a nearby road. The sign read, "Warning—900-foot Jesus Crossing."

The end result of the administrative proceeding was that the OHPC granted the CON to City of Faith Hospital. Bill said, "Their action may or may not have been more political than judicial, but if votes counted, then clearly the City of Faith had the great advantage with 400,000 letters of support." [10]

The first level of appeal from the OHPC decision was to the District Court of Tulsa County where the case was assigned to Judge Ron Ricketts, whom Bill considered to be one of the finest state judges on the bench. The job of the district court was to look at all the evidence and make a de novo decision based upon the record of testimony at the administrative hearings. Both sides wrote briefs and argued the case to Judge Ricketts.

The judge agreed with Bill's legal position on both principal issues. Ricketts found that there was no need for additional hospital facilities in Tulsa and the application, if granted, would be in contravention of the Establishment Clause of the First Amendment to the United States Constitution.

Bill thought the decision of Judge Ricketts was courageous, quite correct, and that the system had worked and justice had prevailed. But another very important issue arose in the trial court. The City of Faith asked the court to stay its judgment pending appeal, allowing the hospital to continue with construction which had already begun. City of Faith lawyers said they knew the risk and that if the Oklahoma Supreme Court agreed with Judge Ricketts, the structure would have to be used for something besides a hospital. Perhaps based upon the assumption of risk statement, Judge Rickets, over Bill's strenuous objection, did grant City of Faith's application for a stay of the judgment while the case was pending on appeal.[11]

Bill's legal team first tried to have the Supreme Court appeal dismissed, arguing that it was premature because Judge Ricketts had remanded the case to the OHPC for further proceedings in accordance with his decision. However, the Supreme Court denied the motion to dismiss. So, Bill and his fellow lawyers began briefing the case and preparing for oral argument.

On March 24, 1981, the Oklahoma Supreme Court, in a 6-3 decision, overruled the district court, holding that greater weight should be given to the findings of the OHPC. The decision said there had been an adequate showing of need for additional hospital beds in Tulsa. The high court also held that the application and plans for City of Faith did not contravene the Establishment Clause.[12]

After the Supreme Court decision was released, Bill met
with the executive officers of the hospitals constituting the
Tulsa Area Hospital Council. They had been through a long
and costly battle where passions ran high. Bill recommended
they authorize his legal team to file a petition for writ of
certiorari in the United States Supreme Court. Bill believed
the nation's highest court might take the case because the
Establishment Clause was involved. Bill also argued that
the speculation that City of Faith would draw patients from
all over the nation was thin. But the decision of the hospital
administrators was to battle no more. They voted to let
the matter end with the Oklahoma Supreme Court's 6-3
decision.[13]

As to the need for a new hospital in Tulsa, the perspective
from a quarter century after the legal fight proved Bill's
clients to be correct. However great the dream, the City of
Faith did not succeed. Patients did not come in significant
numbers from around the nation. The hospital lost money. It
continued to operate based upon support of television appeals
made through Oral Roberts Ministries. But this support
was temporary and diminished, perhaps in part because of
scandals involving other television ministries. The scandals
never involved anyone connected to Oral Roberts, but the
serious problems of some seemed to affect other ministries.

The City of Faith Hospital closed after nine years of
operation and the medical school established as part of
the grand proposal moved to another institution outside
Oklahoma.

Silkwood

*The circumstances of Karen Silkwood's death will always
remain a mystery. Whether she intentionally contaminated
herself with plutonium to embarrass her employer or whether
she was murdered to prevent the employer's embarrassment
will be discussed for generations.*
—From a British Broadcasting Corporation (BBC) documentary

The Oklahoma Highway Patrol has investigated thousands
of single vehicle accidents in its history. However, none
became as famous, or infamous, as a tragic accident that
happened in the darkness along a lonely stretch of Oklahoma
Highway 74 a few miles south of Crescent, Oklahoma, on
November 13, 1974.

When the state trooper arrived at the scene of the
accident, he found 28-year-old Karen Silkwood dead. She
was alone in her white Honda Civic. From the broad, two-
lane asphalt road, it appeared to the officer that Silkwood
had veered to the left, crossed the highway, went off the

road, and hit a concrete culvert head on. A few weeks before, Silkwood had similarly left the road into a barrow ditch, but she escaped without injury when her vehicle came to a stop without striking any object.[1]

The investigating officer found one or two tablets of the sedative, methaqualone, in the car and a small amount of marijuana. The official police report concluded that Silkwood fell asleep at the wheel. There was no firm evidence of foul play. No glass or other debris was found, ruling out any hit-and-run theory.

An autopsy showed Silkwood had a therapeutic dose of methaqualone in her bloodstream and a rather massive dose in her stomach that had not yet reached the bloodstream. At the time, methaqualone was a regulated substance which was popular in the world of "recreational drugs." On the street, it was called a "qualude" or "lude." The drug was prescribed to relieve tension and induce sleep. Medical literature admonishes the user of the drug not to operate a motor vehicle.[2]

Silkwood had a legal prescription for the drug, but had obtained prescriptions from more than one doctor to obtain more than the prescribed dose. Neither the results of the autopsy or facts of Silkwood's prior similar accident shortly before her fatal wreck were admitted into evidence in the later trial. The jury was never aware of either set of facts.[3]

Silkwood was a young divorcee, quite intelligent, who had previously lived in the Duncan, Oklahoma area. Her husband won custody of three children in the divorce proceeding and she moved to the Oklahoma City area. She landed a job as a laboratory technician at the Kerr-McGee

Corporation plant near Crescent that fabricated plutonium fuel pins for the federal government. The plant was constructed on a bluff overlooking the Cimarron River on Oklahoma Highway 74.

After being hired at the plant, Silkwood became an active member of the Oil, Chemical & Atomic Workers Union (OCAW) local. She took part in a strike and was elected to the union's bargaining committee. She also was assigned to investigate health and safety issues. She openly criticized Kerr-McGee for alleged violation of health regulations, including exposure of workers to nuclear contamination, faulty respiratory equipment, and improper storage of samples.[4]

In the summer of 1974, Silkwood traveled to Washington, D.C., to discuss alleged safety violations with national officials of the OCAW which was negotiating a new labor contract with Kerr-McGee. While in the nation's capital, she testified at a hearing before the Atomic Energy Commission (AEC) and repeated her accusations of poor safety standards at the Kerr-McGee Cimarron facility.[5]

Back in Oklahoma, Silkwood began looking for evidence of safety violations and agreed to meet with newspaper reporters. On November 5, 1974, Silkwood performed a self check and found some plutonium contamination on her hands and arms. She was decontaminated and sent home. Two days later, when she reported for work, she was found to have significant amounts of plutonium on her person, despite leaving the plant free of contamination the day before.[6]

Later testing revealed that her apartment was heavily contaminated and urine samples which Silkwood had collected were contaminated. Experts believed the samples had been spiked with plutonium which had not been naturally secreted. Kerr-McGee decontaminated her apartment and sent her to the Los Alamos scientific laboratory in New Mexico to undergo tests concerning her contamination.[7]

Silkwood reported back to work on November 13, took part in a union negotiation session, met with AEC inspectors about her contamination, and attended a union strategy session. The union had arranged for Silkwood to meet with a New York Times reporter, David Burnham, and a national union leader, Steve Wodka, that evening. It was on the way to the meeting that Silkwood died in the automobile accident.

Officials of the OCAW hired an investigator to look into the circumstances of Silkwood's accident. The investigator said there was a trace of blue paint on one of the rear fenders of Silkwood's vehicle. That statement fueled speculation that a Kerr-McGee vehicle may have run Silkwood off the road. The company's colors were blue and yellow and some of its vehicles were painted those colors.

A media frenzy began—and lasted for years. Certain myths, not based upon fact, were kept alive by the media and came to be accepted as truth by a large segment of the public. Silkwood became the idol of many who were strongly opposed to nuclear energy.

Nearly two years after Silkwood's death, a lawsuit was filed in federal court in Oklahoma City against Kerr-McGee Corporation and all its principal officers and directors. The suit was filed by Silkwood's father, William M. Silkwood, on behalf of his daughter's estate and her three children.[8]

Two claims were asserted. First, that Silkwood's civil

rights had been violated by the company and its management as part of a conspiracy among big corporations such as Kerr-McGee and the Federal Bureau of Investigation and other law enforcement agencies. Second, the lawsuit alleged that Kerr-McGee was responsible for Silkwood's personal injury due to plutonium contamination. There was never an allegation that Kerr-McGee or its management was responsible for the automobile accident in which she died.[9]

The attorney in the Kerr-McGee legal department in charge of litigation was Derrill Cody, known as a fine legal mind and a delightful person to work with. Prior to the filing of the Silkwood case, Crowe & Dunlevy performed a significant amount of legal work for Kerr-McGee and Bill was one of the lawyers assigned to several of the matters.

Shortly after the Silkwood case was filed, Cody visited Bill's office and asked him to represent the company and the directors and officers in the litigation. In that conversation, Cody shared a conversation he had had while Vip Crowe was still alive. Cody asked Crowe who he should talk to at the law firm when Kerr-McGee was faced with a major lawsuit. Crowe's answer was, "Bill Paul." So, even after Crowe's death, Bill continued to benefit from his relationship with Crowe.[10]

The Silkwood case was first assigned to United States District Judge Luther Eubanks. It was apparent to Bill and other observers that the case was being financed by the Natural Resources Defense Council (NRDC), a large, well-known environmental group whose concerns about nuclear energy were well publicized. One of the NRDC staff attorneys was assigned fulltime to the case and took numerous depositions. Kerr-McGee produced thousands of pages of documents.[11]

The Silkwood lawyer could find no evidence and had only unsubstantiated claims. At one hearing, Judge Eubanks became so impatient with the lawyer that he said, in open court, "Your case does not amount to a hill of beans!" Shortly thereafter, Judge Eubanks voluntarily disqualified himself from hearing the remainder of the case which was then assigned to another Oklahoma City federal judge, Luther Bohanon.

At first, Silkwood's legal team was pleased that the case was assigned to Judge Bohanon who was known for enforcing claims of civil rights violations if he thought the facts justified such a finding. Bohanon had been extremely controversial in previous decades when he ordered integration of Oklahoma City's public schools and placed the operations of the state prison system under court supervision for alleged civil rights violations.

With a new judge on the case, many motions were filed and set for hearing. After oral argument, Judge Bohanon sustained all of Kerr-McGee's motions. Quickly, Silkwood's lawyer filed a motion to disqualify Judge Bohanon on the basis that his federal bench appointment had been sponsored by the late United States Senator Robert S. Kerr, one of the founders of Kerr-McGee. There was no hearing on the motion, but the United States Court of Appeals for the Tenth Circuit (Tenth Circuit) assigned Frank Theis, a federal district judge from Wichita, Kansas, to the case.

Judge Theis gave the plaintiff additional time and opportunity to come up with evidence to support the claims.

The judge sustained Kerr-McGee's motion to dismiss plaintiff's claims of civil rights violations.[12] The Tenth Circuit affirmed the decision and the officers and directors of Kerr-McGee were dismissed from the case.[13] The individuals had been named as defendants only in the civil rights violation claims.

Media attention to the Silkwood case was enormous. A graduate student from the University of Southern California, Buzz Hirsch, attended most of the depositions and hearings. Bill discovered during one deposition that the contents of Silkwood's automobile had been turned over to Hirsch. Bill and his legal team sought to obtain the contents.[14]

The Writers Guild of America and the Motion Picture Association of America came to Hirsch's aid and argued that Hirsch was working for a production company in an effort to make a factually accurate documentary film and had promised confidentiality to those who gave the contents of the automobile to him. Judge Eubanks agreed with Kerr-McGee and ordered the items produced. However, the Tenth Circuit disagreed, holding that Hirsch's First Amendment right may be violated by being forced to hand over the materials.[15]

Hirsch later was the executive producer of a major motion picture, "Silkwood," that was nominated for an Oscar in several categories. When Hirsch was in the early stages of producing the movie, he requested a half-day of Bill's time to talk about the case. Bill received permission from Kerr-McGee to talk to Hirsch. At the outset of the interview, Bill jokingly said he would talk to Hirsch only if he promised Robert Redford would play Bill in any subsequent movie.[16]

Redford never appeared in the movie but other major

stars did. Meryl Streep played the part of Karen Silkwood, Cher played the part of Sherri Ellis, Silkwood's roommate, and Kurt Russell played the part of Drew Stephens, Silkwood's boyfriend. The movie, which 30 years later appears regularly on television movie channels, ends in the death of Silkwood—the trial is not included.

Despite all the media attention, Bill and two other lawyers at Crowe & Dunlevy continued to prepare the case for jury trial in the event that the plaintiff was allowed to proceed on the remaining personal injury claim. L.E. "Dean" Stringer and John J. Griffin, Jr., assisted Bill on a full-time basis on the Silkwood case. Stringer was familiar with the case because he had assisted Vip Crowe on some of the incidental legal problems associated with Silkwood's death in the two years before the federal lawsuit was filed. It was a demanding assignment for Stringer and Griffin, but Bill was pleased with their efforts.[17]

Bill Zimmerman replaced Cody as head of litigation in Kerr-McGee's legal department and joined the legal team for the corporation. Bill believed Zimmerman brought a great deal of legal talent to the table and Kerr-McGee was fortunate to have his expertise.

With the alleged civil rights violations gone from the case, plaintiff's counsel turned their attention to the personal injury action for which damages were claimed due to plutonium contamination. It was undisputed that Silkwood had become contaminated and that her apartment was contaminated. Kerr-McGee's theory of the case, which Bill felt was the most plausible under the circumstantial evidence, was that Silkwood had intentionally spiked her urine samples with plutonium to which she had access in the laboratory where she worked. Bill believed Silkwood wanted to embarrass Kerr-McGee on this critical safety issue during negotiations with the union.[18]

Although not a position advanced in the trial, the feeling of those who supported Silkwood and her cause was that Kerr-McGee had Silkwood murdered to prevent her from blowing the whistle on safety violations at the Cimarron facility.

Kerr-McGee's theory later received an unlikely endorsement in Richard Raske's book, *The Killing of Karen Silkwood*. According to Raske, security was so lax at the Kerr-McGee plant that workers could easily smuggle out finished plutonium pellets. One of the persons interviewed by Raske for his book reported that Silkwood had once asked what would happen if someone ate a plutonium pellet.[19]

There was no doubt that Silkwood had been assigned the responsibility of coming up with proof of safety violations and was under pressure to do so. When her urine samples were tested, she knew they would show a high level of plutonium, thereby creating an embarrassing situation for Kerr-McGee. When Silkwood first reported to work after allegedly contaminating herself and her apartment, she was asked by the chief health technician how that could have happened. Silkwood told the technician that she had spilled her urine sample in the bathroom of the apartment.[20]

At the Los Alamos laboratory, tests results showed that Silkwood had between 25 and 50 percent of the permissible lifetime body burden of plutonium contamination allowed by the AEC for plutonium workers. In other words, by AEC standards, she was well within the levels of safety and had sustained no cognizable injury.[21]

The plaintiff's theory was that, because plutonium is a hazardous substance and because the law requires absolute liability from anyone handling hazardous materials, it did not matter how it happened, and Silkwood's estate was entitled to recover for any personal injury sustained. At the trial, plaintiff's counsel was fond of saying, "If the lion gets away, Kerr-McGee must pay."

In addition to contending that Silkwood was not injured, Kerr-McGee raised two legal defenses. First, because Silkwood was a Kerr-McGee employee, her sole remedy was under the Oklahoma workers' compensation laws and that the Oklahoma Workers' Compensation Court had sole jurisdiction of the personal injury claim. Second, that as a matter of law, nuclear energy operations were under the exclusive regulation of the federal Atomic Energy Commission and that Silkwood's estate could not maintain a claim under Oklahoma's personal injury laws.[22]

As the Silkwood case neared the jury trial stage, Kerr-McGee's insurance carrier requested that its own lawyers participate in the trial. Elliott Fenton of Oklahoma City was tabbed by the insurance company and joined the legal team. He was assisted by Larry Ottaway, a young litigation associate in the firm. Bill was lead counsel but divided many major trial responsibilities with Fenton, whose reputation as an excellent and seasoned trial lawyer preceded him.

Bill and the team of lawyers worked day and night preparing witnesses and documentary evidence for what would become the longest civil trial in Oklahoma history.

A
MEDIA CIRCUS

And thus ended the 11-week federal court trial in Oklahoma City
that had become the nationwide cause celebre of
anti-nuclear activists, environmentalists, women's rights activists,
and the labor movement.
—The Daily Oklahoman

The Silkwood case was set for trial in March, 1979. Two months before the jury trial was to begin at the federal courthouse in Oklahoma City, plaintiff's counsel arranged for Gerald S. "Gerry" Spence to become the lead lawyer. Spence was a flamboyant and charismatic lawyer from Wyoming who had experience as a prosecutor and insurance company defense lawyer. After he "saw the light," he switched sides and began representing injured clients against the insurance companies he once worked for.[1]

Spence assumed only a small role in the pretrial work—his obvious worth to the plaintiff's case was his performance in the courtroom. He had outstanding communication skills. He wore Western garb with a fringed jacket and a big hat,

and loved the attention of the media—and there was plenty
of that. He was entertaining and very effective with a jury.
He was particularly adept at cross-examining witnesses. If a
witness had a weakness in his or her testimony, Spence could
sniff it out, exploit it. Bill remembered, "What started as a
tiny scratch would wind up as a severed artery." [2]

Even though Spence was effective in the courtroom
from day one of the trial, he, in Bill's opinion, was "very
unprofessional and pursued a course of conduct which was a
discredit to the legal profession." [3]

Outside the presence of Judge Theis, Spence would
address opposing counsel "in the most profane way" and
would engage in ridicule. On one occasion, well into the trial,
Spence, even though he had repeatedly been admonished
to cease improper tactics, nevertheless crossed the line of
proper trial methods. Bill objected, as he had before, and the
judge sustained the objection, as he had before. However, 30
minutes later, Spence was at it again.[4]

Bill asked Judge Theis to admonish Spence in front of
the jury. In a private conference at the bench, the judge said
it was a rare occasion when he would admonish a lawyer
for improper conduct in front of a jury, but that it appeared
this was the only way he could make a point. "Spence then
became as a child," Bill remembered, "asking forgiveness,
and literally begged the judge not to dress him down before
the jury. He succeeded in talking the judge out of it, but the
next day he was at it again." [5]

One of Spence's many egregious actions occurred near
the end of the plaintiff's presentation of evidence. The judge

had ordered counsel to get together over a weekend to discuss certain issues. At that meeting, Spence asked Bill to give him the names of his first few witnesses that would appear for the defense. Bill had made the same request from Spence before the plaintiff's case had begun and Spence had refused. At that time, the judge ordered the parties to supply a list of witnesses two days before a particular witness would be called. So, Bill said, "The two-day rule is in place and I will follow it. I will give you the same consideration you gave me." [6]

Spence exploded and cursed Bill. Bill was not surprised. Because he had been ordered to meet with Spence, he could not just get up and walk out, but he simply wrote down everything Spence had said. Bill's plan was to file a complaint with the appropriate bar association if Kerr-McGee won the case. At the same time, he did not plan to file a bar complaint if his client lost. He did not want any complaint to have the appearance of "sour grapes." [7]

Bill believed Spence knew he had gone far beyond the parameters of professional behavior and was concerned about what Bill might do about it. So Spence, in typical fashion, mounted a first-strike strategy. In the first meeting with the judge the following Monday morning, Spence said he had a matter of ethics he wanted to present concerning Bill's conduct. That was a surprise to Bill who could not wait to hear what Spence had to say. Bill knew unequivocally he had not violated any ethics rule.[8]

Although they were weeks into the trial, Spence charged that Bill had gone beyond the bounds of the rules

of professional conduct in the opening statement. He asked
the court to review it and take appropriate action. Bill said,
"I knew what Spence was doing. He was posturing to be
the first to complain about conduct so that if I charged him
with improper conduct, it would appear that it was only in
retaliation for his allegations about me." [9]

Two days later Judge Theis said he and his law clerks had
carefully reviewed the transcript of Bill's opening statement,
had found nothing wrong with it, and that Spence's charges
were without merit.

The Silkwood case was tried under very difficult
circumstances. Bill lost 13 pounds during the trial. Although
Judge Theis had ruled in Kerr-McGee's favor on the civil
rights violation allegations, his rulings were almost uniformly
against Kerr-McGee in the personal injury case. He ruled
against the corporation on the workers' compensation
exclusivity issue, on which Kerr-McGee later prevailed on
appeal, and on almost every evidentiary controversy.[10]

Instead of being limited to a case about Karen Silkwood
and her injuries, the judge permitted the scope of the trial
to be about the entirety of the operations of the Cimarron
facility. Proceedings in the case were reported daily on radio
and television and were front-page material in newspapers.

The coverage went beyond Oklahoma's borders.
Nationally, it was the time during the high water mark of
anti-nuclear activity. Anti-nuclear protests were being held in
all parts of the country and activists had been successful in
shutting down construction of every planned nuclear plant,
including the Black Fox plant in northeast Oklahoma.

During the first week of the trial, Jane Fonda appeared on the "Mike Wallace Show" on national television and blasted Kerr-McGee's role in Silkwood's death. The national television networks followed the case and reported on it at least several times a week. Shortly before the final arguments to the jury, the largest anti-nuclear demonstration to that time in history was held in Washington, D.C. Thousands marched in the streets under the leadership of Fonda and Tom Hayden. The demonstration was front page material for the nation's newspapers.

If the adverse publicity were not enough, in the middle of the fourth week of the trial, an accident at the nuclear electric power generation plant at Three Mile Island, Pennsylvania, occurred. A nuclear reactor suffered a partial core meltdown. The accident unfolded over the course of the next five days and was the lead story on the nightly news. It was billed as the world's worst nuclear disaster, although the reactor was brought under control and no injuries were ever reported. But the accident furthered a major decline in the public popularity of nuclear power.[11]

The Three Mile Island accident came only a few days after the release of a controversial movie, "The China Syndrome," which featured Jane Fonda as a news anchor at a California television station. In the film, a nuclear accident almost happens while Fonda and her film crew are at a nuclear power plant doing a series on nuclear power. When the film was released, Fonda began publicly speaking out against nuclear power.[12]

The avalanche of anti-nuclear publicity caused Bill and

his fellow Kerr-McGee lawyers to file a motion for mistrial. Judge Theis denied the motion because he said he was confident the jury was not watching news coverage or reading about the Three-Mile Island incident, because he had told them not to.

The closing arguments to the jury took more than eight hours. Bill told the jury that the union had "put an awful pressure on that girl and that Karen was flunking out trying to find that the fuel pins were not good." About Kerr-McGee's allegations that Silkwood spiked her own urine samples to embarrass the company, Bill said, "There is overwhelming evidence that Karen Silkwood did it. There is no evidence that anyone else did it." [13]

A newspaper reporter observed that Bill alternately painted Silkwood as victim and as a schemer "spying" on her employer. Bill said, "Kerr-McGee never did anything wrong to Karen Silkwood. She did something wrong to us by trying to embarrass the company." [14]

The jury deliberated for more than three days. The verdict was not good news for Kerr-McGee. The jury awarded $500,000 in damages for plutonium contamination for the nine-day period preceding Silkwood's death and awarded $10 million in punitive damages to punish Kerr-McGee. The jury also awarded $5,000 as the stipulated value of property in her apartment that had to be destroyed because it was contaminated with plutonium.

As with the coverage of daily events in the trial, the jury verdict was a major news story around the world. A reporter for *The Daily Oklahoman* wrote:

The tense silence in the crowded courtroom was pierced by the cry of a baby, quickly hushed. When the verdict was read…gasps and whispers filled the air.

When the bailiff announced the damages…there were those among the 200 people who swore they heard thunder roll above the skylight. And when U.S. District Judge Frank G. Theis excused the six-man, six-woman jury that had deliberated for four days, half the room came to its feet to cheer the panel's decision. [15]

Bill was extremely disappointed because he did not believe justice had been done, and he said, "I hated to lose." [16] When he returned to his office, he had a call from a good lawyer friend from Clinton, Oklahoma, Pepper Meacham. When Bill informed Meacham about the verdict, Meacham, known for seeing the bright side of any situation, asked how much the Silkwood estate was seeking in the lawsuit. When Bill informed Meacham that they were asking for $70 million in damages, Meacham said, "Well, look at it this way. You didn't lose $10 million—you saved $60 million!" [17]

Judge Theis overruled Kerr-McGee's post-trial motions and wrote a lengthy opinion supporting his decision.[18]

Shortly after the trial, Bill met with Dean McGee, chairman and chief executive officer of Kerr-McGee Corporation, about appealing the case. Bill told McGee that he deeply regretted the jury verdict but was convinced that the legal positions taken by the defense team were strong. Bill gave McGee the opportunity to replace him with other counsel during the appellate process. McGee said, "Absolutely not. You and your firm want to win this case as badly as we do. We will put all the resources necessary into the case to finally prevail." [19]

Two additional law firms joined the defense team, at the request of Kerr-McGee and its insurance carrier. The firms were Chadwell, Kayser, Ruggles, McGee & Hastings of Chicago and Steptoe & Johnson of Washington, D.C.

Bill and Glenn W. McGee of the Chadwell Kayser firm argued the case before the Tenth Circuit on November 17, 1980. Gerry Spence did not appear at oral arguments for the Silkwood estate.

Bill told the appeals judges that the trial was conducted in an atmosphere of "hysteria" because of the Three Mile Island accident and that Silkwood attorneys had capitalized on that hysteria to win an overly large punitive damage award. Bill also said Judge Theis's refusal to poll the jury on their reaction to the Three Mile Island accident alone was grounds for reversal of the judgment.[20]

Bill also argued that the case should never have proceeded in federal court. After all, Bill said, it was a simple workers' compensation case if Silkwood was claiming injuries from work-related activities.[21]

On December 11, 1981, 13 months later, the Tenth Circuit handed down its decision. Kerr-McGee achieved nearly a total victory in the case. The Tenth Circuit held that Judge Theis should have granted judgment in favor of Kerr-McGee on the personal injury issue because workers' compensation was the exclusive remedy for injuries Silkwood may have sustained and that punitive damages could not be awarded against Kerr-McGee because of federal preemption

of regulation of the nuclear industry. The court left standing
the jury's award of $5,000 for the loss Silkwood's possessions
when her apartment had to be destroyed.[22]

The Silkwood Estate appealed the Tenth Circuit decision
to the United States Supreme Court. Lawyers for Silkwood
did not contest the decision that the personal injury action
was covered by workers' compensation laws but did argue
that federal law should not take precedence over state tort law
as it related to punitive damages. Lee Cook of the Chadwell
Kayser firm argued the case before the high court.

On January 11, 1984, the Supreme Court decided, in a
five to four decision, that federal law did not preempt state
tort law on the issue of awarding punitive damages. Justice
Lewis Powell, one of Bill's legal heroes, wrote a dissenting
opinion that supported Kerr McGee's view of the facts and
applicable law.[23]

The effect of the Supreme Court decision was that the
$5,000 property damage award remained intact and the Tenth
Circuit was to further determine if any punitive damages
might be awarded in connection with the small property
damage recovery. Bill continued to lead the appellate team on
briefs filed with the Tenth Circuit. The crux of Kerr-McGee's
position was that judgment should be entered for Kerr-McGee
on the punitive damage issue because there was no evidence
that contamination of Silkwood's apartment was caused by
any malicious or wanton conduct.

Bill's active involvement in the case ended in December,
1984, when he accepted the offer of Phillips Petroleum
Company to become its general counsel. Peter Nickel of the

Covington & Burling law firm in Washington, D.C., was hired to replace Bill as lead counsel for Kerr-McGee. L.E. Stringer and John Griffin of Crowe & Dunlevy remained in the case, working with Nickel.

On July 31, 1985, the Tenth Circuit ruled that the case be returned to the federal district court for a new trial, with instructions that the entire focus of the trial be on the type of conduct by Kerr-McGee, and if such conduct could have caused damage to Silkwood's property.[24]

Even though Bill was no longer actively involved in the defense of the case, he was consulted about the possibility of a new trial by Kerr-McGee's general counsel, Tom McDaniel, now the president of Oklahoma City University. Bill supported the economic decision to settle the nearly decade-long litigation for approximately $1.3 million. Bill said, "Although I continued to believe there should be no recovery of any punitive damages, I felt it was a wise decision to avoid the great expense of another trial and to put an end to this very troublesome case." [25]

*Bill was a businessman's lawyer. He would help you do the right
thing. He wasn't afraid to tell us when our plans were simply the
wrong way to go about conducting business.*
—C.J. "Pete" Silas

*I*n June, 1984, "out of the blue," a representative of Phillips
Petroleum Company (Phillips) contacted Bill to see if he
would be interested in becoming general counsel of the oil
and gas giant.   Bill had handled a case for Phillips a few
years before, but knew little about the company's operations,
although he was acquainted with some of the executives and
lawyers for the company.[1]

Phillips traced its roots to its headquarters city,
Bartlesville, Oklahoma, where Frank Phillips and his brother,
L.E., hit their first gusher in 1905, the first of 81 wells without
a single dry hole. Phillips had long been a leader in the
petroleum industry. In 1923 the company won its first patent
on a process for recovering natural gasoline from natural gas.
In 1929 Phillips was the first company to develop and market

propane for home heating and cooking. Phillips scientists invented polyethylene plastics in 1951 and was the first American oil company approved to drill for oil in Alaska.[2]

Bill's first response to the Phillips' inquiry was that he probably would not consider a move, but he asked for a few days to consider the possibility. He carefully analyzed a stack of materials about Phillips and its management and goals.

Phillips was the largest corporation based in Oklahoma, and 15th largest of the Fortune 500 companies. It had about 25,000 employees and conducted business on every continent except Antarctica. The legal department consisted of 85

Bill's mother, Helen Paul, and her grandchildren in December, 1982. Left to right, Elaine, George, Jamie, Alison, Helen, Lela, Charles, Jennifer, and Steve. *Courtesy Bill and Barbara Paul.*

lawyers in offices in Bartlesville, Oklahoma City, Houston, Amarillo, Denver, and Huntington Beach, California, in the United States. European legal offices were located in Stavanger, Norway; London, England; and Brussels, Belgium. A lone Asian office was located in Singapore.[3]

In addition to attorneys in Phillips's operations offices, more than 20 lawyers supported the company's Research and Development department in Bartlesville. Phillips had a rich history of fostering inventions for application in the oil and gas industry and held hundreds of valuable patents in the petrochemical field, primarily in the development of plastics.[4]

The more Bill learned about Phillips, the more he became interested in becoming the chief legal officer of a company doing business worldwide. There was no doubt it would be fascinating because Phillips' operations involved so many areas of law. Bill had experience managing a legal operation—he had served as managing partner of Crowe & Dunlevy for nearly six years in the 1970s. At the time, the law firm was about the same size as the Phillips legal department.

Bill had to consider more than just changing jobs. Any move from Oklahoma City would have a huge impact upon his entire family. He and Barbara discussed the possible move at length. She graciously said she would abide by whatever decision he made. That was not an easy concession on her part because a move to Bartlesville would mean a dramatic change in her life. The Pauls still had two children at home. Elaine was a senior at Casady School and was scheduled to graduate in June, 1985. Stephen was in the eighth grade at Casady.[5]

The economic factor was not a major consideration. By 1984, with new compensation principles in place at Crowe-Dunlevy, Bill was the senior producer, drew the highest income of the firm's partners, and continued to achieve his personal goal of bringing more income into the firm than he took out in earnings. His annual earnings at Crowe-Dunlevy were more than the beginning base salary offered by Phillips, but the Phillips compensation arrangement included incentive plans which could result in additional compensation. Bill's analysis was that, in the short term, he would have less spendable income with Phillips, but probably more in the long term.[6]

In trying to come to a decision, Bill spent time with William C. "Bill" Douce, the company chairman and chief executive officer, and C.J. "Pete" Silas, destined to succeed Douce who had announced he would retire in May, 1985.

Bill liked Silas very much. Silas had graduated with a degree in chemical engineering from Georgia Tech University and joined Phillips in 1953. During his 41 years with the company he served all over the world, including stints as Phillips senior operations officer in Europe and Africa. Bill saw him as a wonderful person and a capable and talented business executive.[7]

Silas had similar feelings about Bill. After extensive interviews and talking with other lawyers and Oklahoma civic leaders about Bill, Silas concluded that Bill was the right man to become general counsel of Phillips. Silas remembered, "In the end, I knew Bill was good for us because of his incredible judgment, experience, and the fact that he always wanted

Bill accepted an invitation from Phillips Petroleum Company to become the energy giant's general counsel in 1984. *Courtesy Bill and Barbara Paul.*

Phillips was a major contributor to the matching funds program at the University of Oklahoma. Presenting a check to OU President Richard Van Horn, center, is Phillips Vice President Ted Sandridge. Bill is at right. *Courtesy Bill and Barbara Paul.*

to do what was right. That was an intangible that we were fortunate to find in Bill." [8]

In October, 1984, Bill accepted the position as general counsel of Phillips, becoming the highest-ranking executive ever brought in from outside the company.[9] It was agreed that the decision would remain confidential until November 1.

Bill wanted his partners at Crowe & Dunlevy to hear it from him. Phillips also wanted to inform its top executives and lawyers. It was agreed that the announcement would be made public on November 1 at 4:00 p.m. Bill was to have a two-month transition period transferring his files to other lawyers but spending some time in Bartlesville, familiarizing himself with Phillips and the legal division, and was to assume his new position on January 1, 1985.[10]

Bill's predecessor as general counsel was Kenneth Heady, a longtime senior executive who had also worked in the gas and gas liquids departments of Phillips. Heady was returning to a senior level position in that area of the company. He was very generous with his time and most helpful to Bill in the transition period. Heady briefed Bill on what he perceived to be the major issues and shared his evaluation of the major pending legal problems of the company. Heady also provided Bill an evaluation of the legal personnel.[11]

The old expression, "A really funny thing happened on the way to the forum," became a reality five weeks after Bill began his transition into his new position. He was in his office at Crowe & Dunlevy on December 4, 1984, when the news broke that T. Boone Pickens, Jr., had targeted Phillips with a hostile takeover bid. Bill Douce called Bill first thing the next morning and said, "We didn't have this in mind when we hired you. This changes everything within our company. If you don't want to come under these circumstances, then you should not. But if you are coming, get yourself up here right now, like this afternoon!"

Bill had already thought about it and felt he had made a commitment to Phillips. The challenge of being on the team to do battle in what surely would be a massive financial struggle seemed to be an experience that very few lawyers would have in their careers. Bill told Douce, "I'm on my way!" Bill went home, packed a suitcase, and did not get back to Oklahoma City until just before Christmas.[12]

The first few days in Bartlesville were spent in planning and strategy sessions with executive management. There was much to do. Pickens was a formidable opponent. He was born in Holdenville, Oklahoma, graduated from Oklahoma State University, began as a wildcatter for Phillips, and became a billionaire as head of Mesa Petroleum which he founded in 1956. Ironically, both Pickens and Bill would later be inducted at the same time into the Oklahoma Hall of Fame.[13]

By 1984, Mesa was one of the world's largest independent oil companies and Pickens shifted his focus to acquiring other oil and gas companies. In addition to trying to take over Phillips in the 1980s, Pickens took on celebrity status as he launched takeover bids for Cities Service, Diamond Shamrock, and Gulf Oil Company.[14]

Upper management at Phillips went into action. Investment bankers had to be engaged to advise the company on the financial aspects of the battle with Pickens. Legal counsel had to be hired, not only for the company but for investment banking firms assisting Phillips. Because Phillips was a Delaware corporation, lawyers had to be hired in New York, Delaware, Washington, D.C., Oklahoma, and Texas. Lines of credit with the company's major lenders had to be arranged. A proxy solicitation firm was hired.[15]

Observing Bill's first actions as general counsel was John L. Williford, general counsel of Phillips' European and African operations. He later became one of Bill's top lieutenants as associate general counsel in the company's headquarters. Williford welcomed Bill's management style, "Having spent his career in a private practice, he brought fresh air. His style of collegiality and consultation had not been possible before in the corporate structure. While he now represented a 'single' client, he still had multiple groups and departments, all with varying interests, priorities, and agendas. That plurality of interest could cause conflict. Rather than become ensnared in such contests, Bill met them with the good will and professionalism for which he is known." [16]

During the early days of the fight with Pickens, the Phillips board of directors had its regular monthly meeting in Bartlesville. Throughout his tenure at Phillips, Bill sat at the table for all board meetings although he was not officially a member of the board.

The December board meeting was Bill's introduction to the prestigious board that included former Secretary of Defense Melvin Laird, former South Carolina Governor and Secretary of Energy Jim Edwards, and Dr. Clark Wescoe, former president of the University of Kansas and chief executive officer of Sterling Drug Company. Wescoe was the longest serving director.[17]

After the first board meeting, Laird, the seasoned political veteran who advised several presidents and served in Congress, told Bill, "I've been involved in four of these takeover battles and my team prevailed in all of them. And

I hope you understand that I don't intend to lose this one."
Laird's words provided additional incentive for Bill to do his
very best.[18]

   For all of December, Heady was still officially general
counsel and had decision-making authority. He and Bill
worked closely as a team. Heady especially involved Bill in
the selection of law firms to represent Phillips in the takeover
battle.

   The investment banking firms retained by Phillips were
Morgan Stanley, in the lead position, and First Boston, in
a support role. Leading the Morgan Stanley team was Joe
Fogg, a highly regarded investment banker and well liked
by the Phillips team. For outside legal counsel in New York
City, Phillips hired the firm of Wachtel, Lipton, Rosen and
Katz. In Delaware, the firm of Arst, Tunnell was hired. In
the nation's capital, Phillips hired Clark Clifford, a former
Secretary of Defense and adviser to four presidents. Clifford,
a former member of the Phillips board, had a long history
of representing the company. In Texas, Morris Harrell of the
Rain-Harrell firm, was retained. In Oklahoma, Harry Woods
at Crowe & Dunlevy became the leader of the Oklahoma
Phillips defense team. Working with Woods were Lloyd
Minter, former Phillips general counsel, of the Boone Smith
firm of Tulsa, and Joe Morris, former federal judge and
former general counsel of Shell USA, of the Goble Gotwals
firm of Tulsa.[19]

   After initial meetings in Bartlesville, the team left for
New York City, setting up headquarters at the Helmsley
Palace Hotel. Meetings were held in a large conference
room at the Wachtel, Lipton offices, just two blocks from the

Bill takes time off from work to take a family hike to the bottom of the Grand Canyon in Arizona. *Courtesy Bill and Barbara Paul.*

Helmsley. Marty Lipton was leader of the outside counsel team. Bill considered him to be a magnificent and brilliant lawyer. Lipton and his partner, Herb Wachtel, had assembled a group of outstanding lawyers and had kept their firm relatively small. Even though the firm had 70 lawyers, it was small compared to most other major New York City law firms.

Bill remembered, "Lipton and his team worked with a determination I have rarely seen." In the early days of the battle it was not uncommon for the lawyers and assistants to work 48 hours non-stop, without sleep. There were thousands of pages of documents to review and thousands more to prepare.[20]

In the Phillips takeover bid, there was more litigation than in Pickens' takeover battles involving Gulf Oil and Cities Service. In a major case in Delaware, Phillips alleged that Pickens had agreed to a "standstill" arrangement in a prior transaction involving General American Oil Company which Pickens had attempted to acquire but which was acquired by Phillips. The documents were somewhat ambiguous, but Bill and Kenneth Heady thought there was substantial merit to the Phillips position. However, the Delaware courts permitted Pickens to proceed. The good thing for Phillips was that the litigation took its toll on the Pickens team and enhanced the posture of Phillips in the fight.[21]

In Oklahoma, a class action suit was filed against Pickens on behalf of the Phillips independent retail service station owners who objected to the proposed acquisition of the company. All the litigation created a "field day"

for lawyers and it kept Heady and Bill extremely busy
supervising and coordinating the complex litigation.

Financing the takeover battle was an expensive
undertaking. The Phillips team fought with conviction and
resolution in the belief that the long-term prospects for the
company were very favorable for the shareholders. Phillips
believed that if Pickens won control of the company, most
likely he would break up the company into several parts
and sell them off as the only way to liquidate the massive
indebtedness incurred as the price of the acquisition.[22]

Ultimately, the battle was resolved by a settlement
concluded in late December. Under the terms of the
agreement, Phillips would convert almost half its equity into
bonds. All existing shareholders were to exchange about 45
percent of their common stock for high-interest coupon bonds
issued by the company. Pickens, who with his associates
in the venture owned about nine percent of the Phillips
common stock, had the same rights as other shareholders.
Also, the Pickens group had the right to "put" their shares
to the company at a negotiated price, a market-based price
predicated on the opinions of the investment bankers. There
was no "green mail" involved.[23]

During the tense time in New York City, Bill spent a lot
of time with Glenn Cox, the Phillips executive vice president
and chief financial officer. As soon as Douce retired, Cox was
scheduled to become president and chief operating officer,
second in command.

Like Pete Silas, Cox was a skilled executive. Cox did his
work usually characterized by a delightful sense of humor.

Bill dressed in long underwear before gearing up for a cold winter day's hunt in South Dakota. *Courtesy Steve Paul.*

Staying at the luxurious Helmsley Palace Hotel bothered Cox who had a well-deserved reputation of being very conservative, even tight. When Cox noted the outrageously high cost of the hotel doing the team members' laundry, he suggested sending the laundry back to Bartlesville on the company plane that was making a daily trip shuttling staff and documents. Cox was convinced that the laundry could be processed much cheaper in Oklahoma.[24]

The reorganization effected by the settlement with Pickens and his associates generated a massive amount of legal work, and as expected, litigation. As general counsel, Bill was preoccupied for the first several months in his new position with the aftermath of the hostile takeover attempt and settlement. Silas made him a member of the management committee that included about a dozen of the senior executives of the company.[25]

Bill did not get the opportunity to get to know the

members of the "in house" legal team until after the hostile takeover attempt was defeated. He found a skilled and competent group of fine lawyers. These included Cliff Roberts, Rufus Bandy, Jim Mullins, John Williford, Charles Griffin, Marion Froehlich, Lou Ottoviani, Ken Rogers, Tom Cubbage, Joe Cochran, Don Jemison, Doug Taylor, Jan Reasor, Charles Daniels, Yves Boone, Elizabeth Harris, Glen Davis, Don Zimmerman, Monty Stratton, Jim Gallogly, Clyde Lea, Mel Bloomfield, Neal Lehman, Chris Cunningham, Dale Billam, and Alan Richmond in the outstanding group of intellectual property and patent lawyers who worked in the Research and Development group.

Under Silas' leadership, it was necessary to change the strategic direction of Phillips. Because billions of dollars of debt was being held by shareholders in the form of bonds, the company had to focus on short-term objectives to quickly generate a lot of cash. Many fine properties that Phillips had acquired over a period of many years had to be sold.[26]

The crude oil markets did not make Phillips' job any easier. At the time of the settlement with Pickens, crude was selling for $28 to $30 a barrel. Within a year, the price dropped to under $10 a barrel. But Phillips survived and later prospered. After the short-term, high coupon bonds, some as high as 14 percent, were retired, the company was able to return to its time-proven long-term strategy. Shareholders in the twenty first century who were shareholders in the mid-1980s have enjoyed generous gains. In 2002, Phillips merged with Conoco and is now known as ConocoPhillips. On a per share basis, the company's stock is now worth more than ten times as much as it was in 1985.[27]

CORPORATE LEGAL HURDLES

The 1,100 lawsuits filed after the Houston chemical plant explosion
could have spelled the end of Phillips Petroleum Company.
—Bill Paul

Shortly after the settlement between Phillips and Boone Pickens, but before the Phillips reorganization plan was implemented, a then little-known and relatively minor player on Wall Street, Carl Icahn, attempted a hostile takeover of the company. The battle in the spring of 1985 did not last long and Icahn was easily brushed aside under the terms of a settlement that was of relatively little significance to Phillips.[1]

Had Icahn's takeover attempt occurred 10 or 20 years later, the battle would not have been so easily won. Icahn went on to become a major player on Wall Street, mounting a successful hostile takeover of Trans World Airlines and becoming a large shareholder in some of the largest companies in the United States.

After the hostile takeover battles, Bill received a great deal of credit for Phillips' successful defense. He said, "I actually received more credit than I deserved, and I was a bit embarrassed about it." On one occasion Bill mentioned his embarrassment to his boss, Pete Silas, who responded, "Bill, take the credit!" [2]

One of the pleasant tasks of the job of general counsel was to visit Phillips' legal offices in Europe. Twice annually, Bill flew to Stavanger, Norway; London, England; and Brussels, Belgium. The largest office in Europe was in Norway because Phillips had major operations in the North Sea in the massive Ekofisk Field. The reserves in the field are mind-boggling. The producing zone is 900-feet thick, and at the high point of production, was pumping more than 550,000 barrels per day, about 50 percent more than the entire state of Oklahoma was producing at the same time.

Production in the Ekofisk Field came from just four platforms about 180 miles off the coast of Norway. Today, seven production platforms continue to pump from 75 meters beneath the North Sea. Production is expected to continue until 2050.[3]

Bill made four trips by helicopter to platforms in the North Sea. It was necessary to wear a heavily-insulated waterproof flotation suit while aboard the helicopter. The North Sea is very cold, and if the helicopter went down, one could not survive more than a few minutes without the survival suit. The production platforms were technological marvels. Phillips made certain the accommodations and food for its work force at sea was excellent. The workers, primarily Norwegian, put in long hours, but were given a lot of time off between tours.

As general counsel, Bill became involved in disputes concerning the production in the North Sea. Phillips was producing in the Ekofisk Field under a concession granted by the Norwegian government which received royalties and taxes. Phillips had several disputes with the government, often involving millions of dollars. Some of the disputes were

The board of directors of Phillips Petroleum Company in 1991. Front row, left to right, Dolores Wharton, C.J. "Pete" Silas, Glenn Cox, and Melvin Laird. Second row, Bill Thompson, Bob Chappell, Dave Tippeconic, Charles Bowerman, and Dr. Jim Edwards. Top row, Bob Froehlich, Norm Augustine, Wayne Allen, Spike Beitzel, Doug Kenna, and Larry Horner. *Courtesy Bill and Barbara Paul.*

Bill and friends on a sea duck hunting trip at Blue Hill, Maine. Left to right, Bruce Felmly, Jack Middleton, Charles Thompson, and Bill. *Courtesy Jack Middleton.*

resolved by negotiations, but others had to be litigated in the Norwegian courts. Phillips hired local attorneys to represent the company in what Bill described as an "independent and fair court system." Phillips only litigated disputes in which it believed strongly in its position. Fortunately, the company won most of its cases in Norway.[4]

One of the great "perks" of traveling in Europe was great food. Bill often visited the Phillips legal office in Brussels and dined with executives of Petrofina, the largest corporation based in Belgium, and a partner with Phillips in producing the Ekofisk Field. The normal lunch meeting among lawyers was in a private dining room with fine wine and some of the best cuisine in Belgium.[5]

In addition to the two hostile takeover attempts, Bill faced two other major legal crises during his tenure as general counsel for Phillips. The first was a patent suit in which Phillips' adversary was duPont Corporation of Wilmington, Delaware. DuPont sued Phillips in federal court in Delaware for infringement of a patent it held on polyethylene, a common plastic substance. Phillips maintained that it was the first to discover or invent polyethylene, that there were defects in the duPont patent application, and that the duPont patent was invalid.

At the time of the trial, legal matters involving patents did not fall under the general counsel's jurisdiction. Instead, lawyers working for the Phillips vice president of research and development handled the case with duPont. To the shock of everyone, the trial judge held that Phillips was infringing on the duPont patent. When Bill reported the decision to Pete Silas, the chief executive officer directed Bill to take charge of the litigation immediately, and "to assign the highest priority to it." If the decision stood, it would cost Phillips hundreds of millions of dollars and require the company to shut down a huge polyethylene production facility located on the Houston, Texas ship channel.[6]

Bill hired trial lawyers from the Kirkland and Ellis firm in Chicago to supplement the Phillips legal team including Fred Bartlit and Don Scott. Phillips first had to obtain a stay order of the trial court decision while it was appealed to the Court of Appeals for the Federal Circuit, a special appellate court based in Washington, D.C. A stay order would prevent the injunction ordered by the trial court from taking effect until the appeal was processed.

The trial court refused to stay its order, forcing Phillips to try something that had never been successfully done—obtain a stay order from the Court of Appeals for the Federal Circuit. Phillips' in-house patent counsel, other lawyers from Phillips, and outside counsel worked around the clock in crisis mode to assemble supporting materials to submit to the appellate court in support of Phillips' application for a stay order. The efforts were rewarded and legal history was made. The appellate court issued the stay order and changed the momentum in the case. The effect was that Phillips was able to continue in the polyethylene business pending appeal and gave the company encouragement about the prospects of appeal. [7]

On the recommendation of Fred Bartlit, Bill selected Phil Beck, a mid-level partner in Kirkland and Ellis, to make the all-important oral argument to the Court of Appeals. Bill had watched Beck in earlier work and thought he had great skill and credibility. Bill watched Beck argue Phillips' appeal before the Court of Appeals. Bill remembered, "It was the best appellate argument I ever heard." Apparently the Court of Appeals agreed, and reversed the trial court. It was a huge victory for Phillips, preventing a devastating loss. Beck has since gone on to national prominence, achieving a reputation as one of the finest lawyers in the country.[8]

The most significant legal crisis during Bill's tenure as general counsel came from the most massive industrial accident in the history of the petrochemical industry. The site of the accident was Phillips' Houston Chemical Complex on

(cutline 131) After Bill and Pete Silas, right, retired from Phillips, Bill spoke at the annual Silas Lecture on Corporate Ethics at Silas' alma mater, Georgia Tech University. *Courtesy Bill and Barbara Paul.*

the Houston ship channel. The accident was caused when liquid ethylene and isobutane under high pressure were accidentally released into the atmosphere above the plant. In just two minutes, several hundreds of tons of hydrocarbons formed a vapor cloud which was ignited. The resulting explosion had the force of several thousand tons of TNT. Twenty four Phillips workers were killed and hundreds more were injured by the explosion. The polyethylene plant where the hydrocarbons were used to produce plastic material was leveled. The loss of life and the physical injuries to the workforce were "horrendous" and the damage to the plant was in excess of $1 billion.

The crisis occurred while Bill was hosting only the third meeting ever of the worldwide Phillips legal team, ironically just across Houston at a conference center. When Bill received news of the tragedy, he immediately drove to the scene. John L. Williford remembered, "His presence was important to the management executives of Phillips. Looking back, it would be difficult to measure the incredible contribution Bill made to the company and its public and legal posture. His leadership from the very beginning would prove invaluable to Phillips." [9]

Within days of the accident, more than 1,100 lawsuits were filed on behalf of the families of the workers who were killed and by workers who were injured. There was no class action suit, but many of the cases were consolidated under a single docket number. Most of the prominent trial lawyers in Texas were involved in the litigation, including Joe Jamail of Houston who had recently represented Pennzoil in a case against Texaco. The huge judgment won by Jamail ultimately forced Texaco into bankruptcy.[10]

Phillips went into action immediately after the disaster. Pete Silas was out of state, but President Glenn Cox flew to the site of the explosion and granted media interviews and represented the company well. Phillips promised a Herculean effort at search and recovery and pledged to assist the affected families.

For the remainder of Bill's six years as general counsel of Phillips, managing the legal exposure of Phillips from the accident was his highest priority. For several years, the accident litigation consumed most of his time. Silas agreed from the outset that Bill, as general counsel, should retain control, rather than give control to outside counsel. Silas promised all the support needed. Bill remembered, "He was good to his word, and did give me backing even when it was not easy for him to do so. Tragedies such as the one we experienced create strains and pressures on a corporate team, and the role of the lawyers in such cases is a difficult one." [11]

Bill restructured the Phillips legal team to handle the crisis. He brought Clyde W. Lea from the London office to work only on the explosion cases in Houston. Lea had to leave his family behind for the first few months. For outside counsel, Bill employed the firm of Fulbright and Jaworski. Blake Tartt of that firm headed a team of excellent lawyers including Otway Denny, Dudley Oldham, and Reagan Simpson. Added to the Fulbright team was Darrell Barger, a great trial lawyer from Corpus Christi, Texas.

Tartt and his fellow lawyers had great respect for Bill's

leadership. Tartt said, "He was a real lawyer's lawyer. We recognized he was one of the top trial lawyers in the nation, so there was never any questioning of his guidance and leadership." Bill had known Tartt since he was president of the Texas Bar Association. The two became even closer friends during the chemical plant explosion litigation.[12]

Bill chaired a weekly meeting of the Phillips' legal team. John L. Williford said, "He was always calm and approached the mountain of litigation in a business-like manner. He demonstrated that he had learned in his previous years to be responsible to his single client with many heads and interests and at the same time successfully conduct the strategy and tactics of a massive and complex legal matter." [13]

Bill traveled to Washington, D.C., to recruit retiring Chairman of the Joint Chiefs of Staff Admiral William Crowe to the University of Oklahoma. Left to right, Dr. John Bozalis, Dean Robert Lusch, Admiral Crowe, Bill, and J.W. "Bill" McLean. *Courtesy Bill and Barbara Paul.*

It was a long and laborious task to work through the cases. Most were settled after months of negotiations. Several were settled during trials. Only two cases went to a jury trial. Fortunately, they were minor cases and the results were favorable to Phillips. When Bill left Phillips on January 1, 1996, only one minor case remained out of the more than 1,100 filed.

Under existing Texas law, there was no cap, or upper limit, on punitive damages in the 24 death cases. Bill was deeply concerned that if any of those cases went to trial, a jury could conceivably award punitive damages in excess of the equity of Phillips, thus eliminating all shareholder value. Bill based his fears on other large punitive damage awards that had occurred in south Texas in previous years.[14]

Clyde Lea and outside counsel settled 23 of the death claims over a period of many months. However, the final case settled only after Bill and Pete Silas personally met with lawyers for the family for negotiations. Phillips had a substantial amount of liability insurance, but not quite enough to cover all the costs of the litigation.

Bill considers the management of the risk and exposure to Phillips in the aftermath of the deadly chemical plant explosion his finest achievement in his legal career. In a worst case scenario, it could have been the end of the company.

After the bulk of the cases were settled, Bill was asked by his good friend who was general counsel of a company larger than Phillips how much the total cost of the litigation had been. When Bill told him, the lawyer said, "I am amazed.

Based upon my experience in Texas, I would have expected
Phillips to have paid twice that amount. Does Phillips know
what an outstanding job you did?" Bill replied, " My good
friends just think that I did my job. Those not so friendly
can't understand how I spent so much money!" [15]

About four years after the accident, Phillips was involved
in a consolidated trial of about 75 of the severe injury claims.
After a week of trial, there was an opportunity to settle
the cases at a figure which Bill recommended. The figure
was tens of millions of dollars and Bill sought authority
from Pete Silas to make the settlements. He also reviewed
it with several other senior executives. One senior officer
said because others had reviewed the recommendation and
supported it, he saw no need to become involved.

But after the settlement, the same senior executive
saw Bill and said, "What went wrong? Why did we pay
out so much money?" Bill was disappointed that the man
would wash his hands of the matter in the decision-making
process, and then come forward to criticize the settlement
after the fact. Bill was tempted to say, "Well, here's what
went wrong. An eight-inch valve in our plant was opened to
the atmosphere, releasing several hundred tons of ethylene
and isobutane; it vaporized, hit an ignition source, exploded,
killed 24 people, injured several hundred, and leveled our
plant. Heavens, man, I thought you had heard!" [16]

Bill, of course, was too classy to make such a response,
but he was extremely disappointed in the conduct of the
otherwise competent and skilled executive who sought to
distance himself from the problem and fault the resolution of

it. That incident was an exception to the rule of teamwork Bill found at Phillips.

Included among the senior executives with whom Bill worked at Phillips were Bob Wallace, Charles Kittrell, Bill Thompson, Dave Tippeconic, Charles Bowerman, John Whitmire, Lynn Rickards, Ken Smalley, Tom Morris, Dr. Joe LeBlanc, Bill Thomas, John Carrig, John Mihm, Gene Bonnell, Jim Mulva, J. Bryan Whitworth, Barbara Price, George Meese, Joe O'Toole, John Van Buskirk, Mike Dabbar, Jack Howe, Ted Sandridge, Dr. Tony Belmont, Ann Cherry, and Roseann Kubicek.

Pete Silas retired in the spring of 1994. Glenn Cox had retired two years earlier and was replaced by Wayne Allen as president. Allen became chairman and chief executive officer upon the retirement of Silas. Many members of the executive team with whom Bill had worked with for a decade retired at about the same time, so Bill worked his final year with a new team. It was not the same as it had been, but Bill tried to adjust to the change as best he could.

Bill retired at Phillips on January 1, 1996, and returned immediately to his old law firm, Crowe & Dunlevy. The 11-year experience at Phillips had been professionally satisfying, challenging, and sometimes stressful, but overall enjoyable. He especially remembered the great people with whom he served and worked at Phillips.

Bill was president of the Oklahoma Bar Association in 1976.
Courtesy Bill and Barbara Paul.

SERVICE TO THE BAR

We cannot change our history. We can shape our future. We are the guardians of the rule of law, which depends for its power on acceptance by the society it governs.
—Bill Paul

One of the highlights of Bill's life has been the opportunity to serve his chosen profession by being active in bar associations and other professional organizations. "Much of what we do in life depends on the mentoring we have had along the way," Bill said. When Bill joined Crowe & Dunlevy in 1957, Raymond Tolbert instilled in him the obligation that lawyers have to do pro bono work and to serve the profession. That lesson was reaffirmed by V.P. Crowe as leader of the firm. Bill remembered, "It was easy for me to become active in the various bar associations because the culture of my law firm encouraged it and supported it." [1]

The first bar office Bill held was in 1963 as president of the Oklahoma County Young Lawyers (OCYL), a group of attorneys age 35 or less. That same year, Paul G. Darrough,

Jr., president of the Oklahoma County Bar Association, asked Bill to serve as treasurer of the county bar. That made him an officer and a member of the board of directors of the county organization.

While president of OCYL, Bill had the opportunity to help break the barriers of segregation. Bill scheduled a luncheon meeting of the organization at the Huckins Hotel in downtown Oklahoma City. One young lawyer was African American and joined his fellow attorneys at the luncheon. Bill was unaware that the Huckins management did not permit African Americans to eat in the dining room. During the luncheon, one of the owners of the hotel came to Bill and irately accused him of "setting us up" by bringing an African American to the meeting.[2]

Bill told the owner he was unaware of the policy, did not agree with it, and that the group would never meet there again. Bill and other OCYL attorneys began a personal boycott of the Huckins and other meeting places that had the same regrettable policy. For a time OCYL held its meetings in the local YWCA that welcomed lawyers of all races. Bill remembered, "Maybe our stand played a small role in area hotels and public meeting places changing their policies." [3]

After serving on the board for several years, Bill was elected president of the Oklahoma County Bar Association (OCBA) for 1971. A principal focus of Bill's leadership was to increase membership and for OCBA to send its own delegate to the American Bar Association House of Delegates. The first person to hold that office was Robert J. Emery, one of Bill's predecessors as president of the county bar organization. Bill and his partner, Andy Coats, also held that position for several years.

A group of former presidents of the Oklahoma Bar Association gathered at an OBA meeting in 2004. Left to right, standing, Douglas Sanders, Andy Coats and wife, Linda, and C.D. Northcutt. Seated, Bill, Barbara, and Ruth Eleanor Northcutt. *Courtesy Bill and Barbara Paul.*

In 1974, Bill ran for president of the Oklahoma Bar Association (OBA). He was elected as president-elect for 1975 and as president for 1976. It was a great experience and enabled Bill to become widely acquainted with lawyers throughout Oklahoma. The legal profession is largely self-regulated and Bill appointed James Sturdivant of the Gable & Gotwals firm in Tulsa as vice president of the OBA to be in charge of disciplinary matters.[4]

One of Bill's projects in his year as president of the OBA was to provide a separate building for the Oklahoma Supreme Court somewhere in the State Capitol complex. He had been impressed by the new Supreme Court building

in Kansas and thought a separate building for the judicial
branch of government in Oklahoma would be supportive
of the principle of independence of the judiciary. "It was
a good idea, but one whose time had not yet come," Bill
remembered.[5]

In advancing the idea, Bill met with leaders of the
Oklahoma legislature and asked the Chief Justice of the
Supreme Court of Kansas to come to Oklahoma and talk
about that state's new court building. Bill met resistance. John
Miskelly, a sage, veteran member of the Oklahoma House
of Representatives, told a reporter, "We don't need a new
building for our old judges. We need some new judges for our
old building." [6]

Bill visits with United States Supreme Court Justice Ruth Bader Ginsberg, center,
and United States Attorney General Janet Reno at a bar association meeting in
1996. *Courtesy Bill and Barbara Paul.*

David L. Boren, a lawyer, was governor of Oklahoma at the time. Bill was visiting with one of Boren's top staff members who said, "The governor wants you to know that as a member of the bar, he supports your idea, but as governor, he did not feel he could take a position. Bill told the governor's assistant, "I would really like it better if he would reverse the two." [7]

Bill began attending annual meetings of the American Bar Association (ABA) in 1961, and has missed only three meetings in the nearly half-century since then. The ABA, now the world's largest voluntary professional association with more than 400,000 members, was founded in 1878 in Saratoga Springs, New York, by 100 lawyers from 21 states. The stated mission of the ABA is "to be the national representative of the legal profession, serving the pubic and the profession by promoting justice, professional excellence, and respect for the law." The official motto of the ABA is "Defending Liberty, Pursuing Justice." [8]

After Bill's year as president of the Oklahoma Bar Association, he became active in the ABA. He was a member of the House of Delegates, the policy-making body of the ABA, as a representative of the state bar, and later as the representative of the Oklahoma County Bar Association. Bill became president of the National Conference of Bar Presidents in 1985. He was general counsel of Phillips at the time, and broadened his circle of friends to include those lawyers serving as general counsel of major corporations in the nation. Bill became active in various corporate counsel organizations.[9]

It was at meetings of the National Conference of Bar Presidents that Bill met Jack Middleton, president of the bar association in New Hampsire. Middleton, who later was president of the same organization, believed Bill's honesty is what made him go so far in life. He said, "He is as honest as the day is long, and people can tell that in a first meeting. He was bright, and his good leadership qualities made him a natural at leading lawyers' groups around the country." [10]

Another state bar president, Stell Huie, of Georgia, was impressed with Bill the first time they got together. He said, "He was obviously a leader, my kind of person. In all the projects we worked on, he focused on the goal until it was accomplished. He was committed to his work, his friends, his family, and to the rule of law." [11]

In 1992, Bill ran for president of the ABA, with the encouragement and support of Phillips' CEO Pete Silas. The campaign was unsuccessful, but Bill said, "I ended the campaign with more friends than I had when I started." That first campaign laid the groundwork for a later successful campaign.

From 1987 to 1995 Bill served as a member of the ABA nominating committee, a group of approximately 60 lawyers from various sections of the ABA. Nomination by the committee for various posts within the ABA was tantamount to election. By serving on the committee, Bill became friends with future leaders of the ABA.

In 1995 Bill was elected to a three-year term on the 35-member ABA Board of Governors, the group that oversees the general operations of the association. Bill retired from Phillips, returned to Crowe & Dunlevy, and received much encouragement to run again for president of the ABA. Several of his friends, Morris Harrell of Dallas; William Falsgraf of Cleveland, Ohio; Roberta Cooper Ramo of Albuquerque,

New Mexico; and Jerome Shestack of Philadelphia, Pennsylvania, had achieved the goal of being elected on a second try, so Bill decided to jump into the race.[12]

Also encouraging Bill was his old friend, Jim Sturdivant, a highly respected lawyer from Tulsa who had served with Bill in the Oklahoma Bar Association and as a member of the ABA nominating committee. Sturdivant, who became Bill's campaign manager, reflected, "There were 67 members of the nominating committee that needed to be contacted. It was not the usual campaign, of speech-making and back-slapping,

Bill's family was present at the Nashville, Tennessee meeting in 1998, where Bill was officially nominated to be president of the ABA. Left to right, Alison Paul Miller, Elaine Paul Seidel, Barbara Paul, Bill, and Steve Paul. Sitting is Bill's mother, Helen Paul. *Courtesy Bill and Barbara Paul.*

Two days before being inducted as president of the American Bar Association, Bill welcomes President Bill Clinton who spoke to the 1999 ABA annual meeting in Atlanta, Georgia. *Courtesy Bill and Barbara Paul.*

Bill accepts the gavel, symbolizing the passing of the title of president of the American Bar Association, from outgoing president Phil Anderson. *Courtesy Bill and Barbara Paul.*

it was one-on-one talks with some of the country's leading lawyers, convincing them that Bill would be the best leader of the honored profession." [13]

Bill received support from his law firm. Jimmy Goodman, Jim Hall, and Gary Davis were active on his behalf. The firm assigned a young associate, Will Hoch, to

Bill, left, presiding over a meeting of the ABA Board of Governors. To his left are Robert Gray of Richmond, Virginia, and Martha Barnett of Tallahassee, Florida. Both later served as president of the ABA. *Courtesy Bill and Barbara Paul.*

devote half his time to assist Bill with his duties after he was elected. Hoch remembered, "From the time Bill hired me, I was in awe of his genuine desire to serve the ABA. He didn't want the title, he wanted to make a difference. I believed in him so much that it was easy to devote long hours to assisting him in contacting some of the major attorneys in the United States to seek their support for his projects." [14]

Another of Bill's supporters was attorney Bill Ross who had been a close friend for decades. Ross said, "He was such a natural because he has always been number one in whatever

Bill and Barbara at Westminster Abbey in London, England, to celebrate the opening of the United Kingdom legal year. As president of the ABA, Bill represented American lawyers at many world events. *Courtesy Bill and Barbara Paul.*

For a fun night, Bill and Barbara hosted the "night of the hat," during an ABA meeting in Chicago. A prize was given for the best hat. *Courtesy Bill and Barbara Paul.*

he did. He is brilliant, is incredibly capable of being a best friend and doing anything for you, and serve his fellow man and the community at the same time." [15]

Bill's opponent for the highest office in the ABA was Thomas F. Smegal, Jr., an intellectual property lawyer from San Francisco, California. Weeks before a February, 1998 nominating committee meeting, it was clear that Bill had the necessary commitments to win the nomination. Smegal withdrew and Bill was nominated by acclamation.

Bill's official nomination came in the ABA mid-year meeting in Nashville, Tennessee. His mother, at age 91, joined Barbara and Bill's four children to witness the event.

Bill's official year as president of the ABA was from August, 1999, through July, 2000. However, in late 1998, as presdent-elect, he began spending much of his time preparing for his presidency. The president of the ABA is the chief executive officer and presides at the meetings of the board. The chief operating officer of the organization is the executive director, a full-time professional who oversees a staff more than 1,200 people. That office was held by Robert Stein of Minnesota.The ABA has two offices, a headquarters in Chicago with approximately 800 people, and a large office with more than 400 staff members in Washington, D.C.[16]

Bill had three principal initiatives as president of America's lawyers—to increase racial and ethnic diversity at all levels of the legal profession, to expand the international rule of law initiatives of the ABA beyond Central and Eastern Europe and Asia to Latin America and Africa, and to harness the new tools of technology, computers and the Internet, to devise more cost efficient ways to deliver legal services to middle and low-income Americans.[17]

Bill felt an urgent need to increase racial and ethnic diversity in the legal profession because of the demographic and population trends in America. In 1999, about 30 percent of the national population was made up of Hispanics, African Americans, Asians, and Native Americans. Experts predicted that by 2050, those groups would make up more than 50 percent of the population, and there would be no "majority" race in the United States.

Bill was alarmed by statistics that showed that less than

eight percent of the country's lawyers came from minority groups. The only profession in the nation that had a smaller percentage of minorities was dentistry.

Bill believed that the issue was crucial for the future of the country. "We are a nation that operates under the rule of law," he said, "If the great majority of our population does not respect the rule of law, it will fail." Bill was strong in his feelings that if racial and ethnic minorities are excluded from the system, from the ranks of judges, prosecutors, and others who administer the law, there is substantial risk they will no longer respect the law." [18]

Bill's first act as president of the ABA was to create what became known as the ABA Legal Opportunity Scholarship Fund. The purpose was to award scholarships to minority students to enable them to attend law school. Bill and Barbara

During his year as president of the ABA, Bill had great assistance from Will Hoch, left, of Crowe & Dunlevy, and Luke Bierman, assistant to the ABA president. *Courtesy Bill and Barbara Paul.*

kicked off the scholarship fund campaign with a $50,000 gift which was matched by Crowe & Dunlevy.[19]

Bill sought support from Oklahoma institutions, and he was pleased with their response. Through Tom McDaniel, Kerr-McGee Corporation contributed $10,000. So did the Gable & Gotwals law firm and the Williams Companies in Tulsa.

With $130,000 in hand, Bill was able to announce the scholarship. The idea caught fire. The Business Law Section of the ABA immediately pledged $115,000, and the Litigation Section trumped that pledge with a $250,000 commitment. By the end of the year, $1.3 million had been raised to fund annual scholarships to 20 of more than 1,000 applicants. Each of the 20 receive $5,000 a year for three years of law school.

At the suggestion of past ABA President Sandy D'Alemberte of Florida, who was then president of Florida State University, the nation's law schools were asked to match the scholarships with a partial tuition waiver. More than half the law schools agreed, three of them matching the scholarship two-to-one. The matching resulted in the scholarships being worth $30,000, and $45,000 at three law schools.

The scholarship program has continued after Bill's service as president. In 2007, 160 minority law students will have received ABA scholarships. Will Hoch, who helped Bill in putting the scholarship program together, said, "It may be Bill's greatest legacy, starting a program that will make it possible for truly outstanding young people to become fine lawyers and great leaders." [20]

In October, 1999, the ABA sponsored a colloquium on racial and ethnic diversity in the legal profession, and the

work product of that meeting remains today as the foundation stone of the work of the ABA in that area. During his term of office, Bill requested each of the several hundred ABA sections and committees to begin each of their meetings with a report of what was being done to increase racial and ethnic diversity in the legal profession.[21]

With his bully pulpit as the leader of the nation's lawyers, Bill spoke frequently about the need to increase diversity. In his "President's Message" to members of the ABA, he wrote:

> *Our profession is more than 90 percent white, and enrollment in our law schools is about 80 percent white. But 30 percent of our society is people of color, and in the next few decades it will be 50 percent. These trends put at risk the profession's historic role as the connecting link between our society and the rule of law...*
>
> *From our ranks come those who foster respect for and understanding of the law—advocates, judges, administrators trained in the law, and a large segment of our civic leaders. Under representation of lawyers of color in our ranks is an institutional weakness and diminishes our capacity to serve.*[22]

MAKING THE PROFESSION BETTER

Bill did not become ABA president for the perks of the office, which are considerable. Instead, he wanted to do something to forever improve the role of lawyers in society.
—James Sturdivant

After successfully launching his first initiative to increase the number of minority lawyers, Bill moved to his second program, to expand the international rule of law initiatives of the ABA. He wrote in the ABA Journal, "The ABA historically has had an international presence, principally through the programs of some of our sections. We should expand the scope and accelerate the pace of those activities." [1]

Bill appointed a special committee headed by immediate past ABA President Phil Anderson of Little Rock, Arkansas, to recommend a structure to enable the ABA to achieve the goal of extending its rule of law initiatives to Latin America and Africa.

Joyce Coleson, left, was Bill's able assistant throughout his American Bar Association leadership experience. Bill said, "Joyce made a significant contribution to my work and that of the ABA." The object around Bill's neck is the ever-present ABA badge or name tag. *Courtesy Bill and Barbara Paul.*

The idea was to build upon an ABA international success story—the Central and East European Law Initiative (CEELI), which had provided technical and legal assistance in 24 countries, including many former republics of the Soviet Union. More than 5,000 lawyers, judges, and law firms had provided free legal assistance in drafting constitutions and civil and criminal codes and establishing independent legal systems and judiciaries in infant democracies.

CEELI had been co-founded by Homer Moyer and Sandy D'Alemberte. United States Supreme Court Justice Sandra Day O'Connor had been active in CEELI from its inception. Justice Anthony Kennedy was involved in a similar council serving countries in Asia.

The Anderson committee recommended the establishment of two new ABA Rule of Law initiative groups for Latin America and Africa. Bill appointed a council for Latin America and asked Justice Stephen Breyer, who was fluent in Spanish, to serve. Justice Breyer agreed and contributed greatly. On the African council, Bill appointed two judges of the United States Courts of Appeals, including his friend, Judge Robert Henry, an Oklahoman, and soon to be Chief Judge of the United States Court of Appeals for the Tenth Circuit.[2]

Bill was pleased with the beginnings of the new initiatives in helping establish judicial systems in other countries. In the ABA Journal, he wrote:

> *As the representative of the American legal profession, the ABA is uniquely positioned to offer helpful advice to developing nations about the foundations of an efficient and effective justice system based on the rule of law…In time, these activities may well prove to be among our most valued achievements.*[3]

The international rule of law initiative remains alive today in the ABA. A restructuring has put all international activity under the umbrella of a single entity with global responsibility. The ABA is committed to helping carry the rule of law into the founding documents and laws of developing nations.

Bill received help in his plan to harness the new tools of technology to more efficiently and cost-effectively deliver legal services from the Law Practice Management Section of the ABA. Bill convened a President's Task Force on Use of Technology for Improving Access to Justice. ABA committees designed Web-based support for practicing attorneys.

The focus of an ABA-sponsored symposium on technology was on e-lawyering, or how lawyers can utilize the Internet as an avenue for developing clients, maintaining an office, and practicing law. The Business Law Section of the ABA developed a Website to assist consumers who shop on the Internet.

Bill opens the 2000 American Bar Association annual meeting in the General Assembly Room at the United Nations headquarters in New York City. *Courtesy Bill and Barbara Paul.*

Bill, left, listens to an address by United States Supreme Court Justice Sandra Day O'Connor, at Runnymeade. *Courtesy Bill and Barbara Paul.*

Bill speaks to reporters about his initiatives as president of the ABA. At right is Luke Bierman, assistant to the ABA president, who greatly helped Bill during his term as head of the ABA. *Courtesy Bill and Barbara Paul.*

Bill's year as ABA president was a year away from home and a year of travel. It was necessary for him to spend a significant amount of time in the ABA offices in Chicago and Washington, D.C. In addition, he traveled throughout the country, making speeches and attending various ABA meetings. During his year, he also traveled outside the United States to Canada, Mexico, Panama, England, France, Germany, the Czech Republic, China, and India.[4]

Barbara traveled with Bill if the trip was two nights or more. She told the ABA staff members who assisted her with schedules and planning, "I don't do one-night stands." The staff was amused by the comment, and several were heard to say, "I don't either!" [5]

Once every 15 years, the ABA adjourns its annual meeting held somewhere in the United States in July or August, and reconvenes in London, to revisit the roots of the common law and of the legal profession. Fortunately, that occurred during Bill's term as president.

The regular New York City annual meeting required much planning. Bill and Barbara and the ABA Host Committee met with Mayor Rudolph Giuliani, a lawyer and member of the ABA. Giuliani was very cordial and cooperative and agreed to special requests for hospitality. The mayor hosted a beautiful reception on the grounds of the Mayor's residence, Gracie Mansion, on the banks of the East River.[6]

Bill presided over the opening ceremonies in the General Assembly Room of the United Nations. The principal address was made by Phil Lader, the American ambassador to Great Britain. Because the ABA meeting was headed to London, it was a relevant and timely speech.

At the dedication of the new ABA memorial at Runnymeade are, left to right, the American Ambassador to Great Britain, Phil Lader, Bill, and United States Supreme Court Justice Stephen Breyer. *Courtesy Bill and Barbara Paul.*

Barbara and Bill pose in front of the inscription Bill wrote for the Magna Carta memorial in England. *Courtesy Bill and Barbara Paul.*

After the ABA House of Delegates concluded its business in New York City, several thousand ABA members headed for England. The first event was at Runnymeade, where King John signed the Magna Carta, considered one of the most important legal documents in the history of democracy. The English charter issued in 1215 influenced modern documents including the United States Constitution and the Bill of Rights.

The only memorial at the site was erected by the American Bar Association. Bill presided over ceremonies at which the main speaker was Justice Sandra Day O'Connor. Each time the ABA meets in England, a stone is taken from the base of the memorial and replaced with a new stone with an inscription. Bill wrote the inscription that was added to the

ABA memorial at Runnymeade:

15 July 2000
The American Bar Association
Returns This Day
To Celebrate Magna Carta
Foundation of the Rule of Law
For Ages Past And
For the New Millennium.

The reference to the new millennium seemed appropriate to Bill because they were meeting in the first year of the millennium. The next planned meeting will be in 2015, the 800th anniversary of Magna Carta.[7]

Bill addressed an ABA meeting in the chamber of the House of Lords in London. Left to right, American Ambassador to Great Britain Phil Lader, United States Supreme Court Justice Anthony Kennedy, Bill, Betty Boothroyd, Speaker of the British House of Commons, and Lord Justice Norse, Master of the Rolls. *Coutesy Bill and Barbara Paul.*

Bill introduced British Prime Minister Tony Blair, left, as the principal speaker at the opening session of the ABA convention in London. *Coutesy Bill and Barbara Paul.*

After the moving ceremonies at Runnymeade, ABA members returned to London for several days of professional meetings and festivities. The opening assembly was a grand occasion at Royal Albert Hall. Bill introduced the principal speaker, British Prime Minister Tony Blair, himself an English barrister. Blair spoke about the role of the United Kingdom in the European community and welcomed American lawyers to his homeland. After the event concluded, Bill had the privilege of talking with the prime minister for several minutes.[8]

Four United States Supreme Court justices, Sandra Day O'Connor, Anthony Kennedy, Ruth Bader Ginsburg, and Stephen Breyer, attended the London meeting. All of the senior judicial officers of the United Kingdom also were there, including the Lord Chancellor, the Lord Chief Justice, the Master of the Rolls, the Chairman of the Bar Council (barristers), and the President of the Law Society (solicitors).

Bill, a long way from the dairy farm in Pauls Valley, is dressed for the opening session of the ABA convention in London, England. *Courtesy Bill and Barbara Paul.*

Several of Bill and Barbara's friends attended the London meeting of the ABA. Bottom row, left to right, Jane Harlow, Billy Bowden, Bill Ross, Lil Ross. Top row, United States District Judge Ralph Thompson, Barbara Thompson, James Sturdivant, and Barbara Sturdivant. *Courtesy Bill and Barbara Paul.*

Two distinguished leaders spoke at ABA luncheons during the meeting. Robin Cook, British Foreign Secretary, spoke about the pressing international issues of the day. Former United States Senator George Mitchell, who had recently successfully mediated an agreement between competing interests in Northern Ireland, was well received. Bill was able to visit with both men prior to their addresses.[9]

Bill's family turned out en masse for the ABA meeting in London. At the closing ceremonies at the Tower of London are, left to right, Karen Paul, George Paul, Alison Paul Miller, Doug Miller, Bill, a Beefeater, Barbara, Darren Seidel, Elaine Paul Seidel, Steve Paul, and Laura Paul. *Courtesy Bill and Barbara Paul.*

The co-chairs of the planning committee for the meeting were ABA Past President Roberta Cooper Ramo of Albuquerque and Peter Goldsmith of London, a distinguished barrister. Peter is now Lord Goldsmith and served as attorney general of the United Kingdom under Prime Minister Tony Blair. Ramo was the first woman to serve as president of the ABA.

The highlight of the trip for many was attending a garden party hosted by Queen Elizabeth II on the grounds of Buckingham Palace. The Queen graciously made about 400 invitations available to ABA members.

Bill and Barbara were honored to be among 50 guests
in the Queen's tea tent to which she and the royal family
repaired after making the rounds greeting hundreds of their
guests. The Pauls and the American ambassador, Phil Lader,
and his wife, were the only Americans present. When the
royal family entered the tent, Prince Phillip approached Bill
and struck up a delightful conversation. He obviously had
been well-briefed on the ABA meeting and some of the issues
we were considering. "I was impressed," Bill said.[10]

When Prince Phillip left, the Queen made her way to
the Americans. After greeting her with traditional courtesies,
Bill told her that the English barristers and solicitors had
been superb with their hospitality and that the ABA was
having a wonderful meeting. The Queen was delighted.
Then, Ambassador Lader said, "Bill, why don't you tell Her
Majesty about the trial of the two Georges?" [11]

The ambassador was referring to the most popular event
at the ABA London meeting which was a mock trial based
on history at the time of the American Revolution. Justice
Stephen Breyer presided over a trial of George Washington
and King George III before a jury of British lawyers. When
Bill told the Queen that Washington was being tried for
treason, she nodded approval, "as if to suggest that he clearly
had it coming to him." [12]

Bill then explained to the Queen that King George III
was being tried in the mock trial for tyranny. The Queen's
visage noticeably changed as she sharply said, "For what?"
Bill softly repeated, "For tyranny, Your Majesty." The

Queen replied, "Good Day!" and turned on her heel and left. Ambassador Lader said, "Well, Bill, it looks like I led you right into that one." In good humor, Lader said, "I think we've just undone the last six months of my work as Ambassador to England." [13]

Two other members of the royal family were in the tent. Bill and Barbara did not get to speak with Prince Charles, but did have an occasion to have a conversation with Princess Anne. They talked about the problems of many years in Northern Ireland, which she and other British citizens referred to as "the troubles." The Pauls found Princess Anne to be down to earth, charming, and pleasant, "without appearing too royal."

Bill reflected on the historic time in the Queen's tea tent, "She and her staff were extremely hospitable and gracious to us. I regretted that she was offended by what everyone else in London seemed to think was a rousing good program. I concluded that Her Majesty is somewhat lacking a sense of humor, but little do I know about the ways of royalty." [14]

An observer of afternoon tea with the Queen was James Sturdivant, whose wife, Barbara, considered her time with the Queen the number one social event of her life. Sturdivant said, "We exercised proper protocol and the men dressed in their finest top hats and tails. I kept thinking, 'For Bill Paul, it was a long way from milking cows in Pauls Valley to having tea with the Queen at Buckingham Palace.'" [15]

The final event of the ABA meeting was an evening reception at the Tower of London, the ancient fortress and prison on the north bank of the River Thames. The first structures were built by William the Conqueror in 1078. For the first time, the entire grounds were reserved for a single event. Guests were able to view the crown jewels, chat with the Beefeaters, examine the executioner's block where so many notables lost their heads, and stroll the bank of the river. [16]

Before the meeting, Bill had voiced his admiration of the exploits of Britain's most famous Naval hero, Admiral Lord Nelson, who was killed during the Napoleonic Wars in the Battle of Trafalgar. At the reception, the commander of the Tower of London presented Bill with a ceramic bust of Nelson.

At the conclusion of the reception, a British Marine band paraded past the Americans. Bill was honored by being in a reviewing stand. Someone obviously told the band director that Bill was a Marine, because as the band marched past him, they began playing the familiar strains of the Marine Corps Hymn. Bill said, "So we concluded the ABA meeting and the evening with 'From the Halls of Montezuma.'" [17]

Following the London meeting, which was attended by all of the Paul children, and their spouses or companions, the European visit for the Paul families moved to France. They traveled by express train through the tunnel under the English Channel and on to Paris. After three days in the French capital, Bill and Barbara went on to Germany as guests of the Bar Association of Germany. They had three fascinating days in Berlin, meeting and visiting with leaders of the German Bar, some of the senior judges, and the mayor of Berlin.[18]

As the whirlwind year as president of the ABA ended,

Bill wrote in his last "President's Message" in the ABA Journal:

> *Time went by so swiftly, and now this bar year ends. There are some things not subject to adequate description. The magnitude of the privilege of serving as ABA president is one of them. You gave me the ultimate gift by permitting me to serve as the leader of our profession. Nothing greater could have ever happened in my professional life. Thank you.*[19]

After serving as president, Bill remained on the Board of Governors for one year as past president and is a member of the ABA House of Delegates for life. Bill continues his service to the profession. Since 2002, he has served as a trustee of the National Constitution Center in Philadelphia. He also has served as a trustee of the American Inns of Court and as a trustee and vice chair of the Center for American and International Law in Dallas, formerly the Southwestern Legal Foundation. He is one of the founding members and served as a director and secretary of the Historical Society of the Court of Appeals for the Tenth Circuit.

In 2004, Bill was presented with the Justice Marian Opala Award for Lifetime Achievement in Law by Oklahoma City University. Left to right, Bill, OCU Law School Dean Lawrence Hellman, and OCU President Tom McDaniel. *Courtesy Bill and Barbara Paul.*

COMMUNITY SERVICE

Bill and Barbara Paul are great examples of giving generously to the University of Oklahoma to assure academic excellence for the future. Their loyalty to OU and its future is unquestioned.
—David L. Boren

Moving back to Oklahoma City after his retirement from Phillips in 1996, Barbara and Bill both became active in the community. In addition to the legal profession, Bill serves his state, his university, and his Native American heritage.

When Brad Henry was elected governor of Oklahoma, he promised to look for just the right position in which Bill could serve the state. One morning in February, 2005, Bill picked up his office telephone before his secretary could. The voice at the other end of the line said, "Bill, this is Brad Henry. I didn't expect you to answer you own phone!" Bill replied, "I didn't expect you to call either!" [1]

The purpose of the call was to ask Bill to do the governor a favor and serve on a seven-member board that

would oversee the state lottery overwhelmingly approved
by Oklahoma voters in November, 2004. Bill told Governor
Henry he would serve—it was not a favor, it was a privilege.

Bill considers his service on the Oklahoma Lottery
Commission a fascinating experience. Under the leadership
of board chairman and distinguished lawyer, Jim Orbinson of
Tulsa, the state lottery was established and "up and running"
in record time. The board had to rent space, buy equipment,
hire staff, and find an executive director. They found James
"Jim" Scroggins, the director of the lottery in Missouri.

Forty five percent of the net proceeds of the Oklahoma
Lottery Trust Fund goes to public schools, kindergarten
through 12th grade. Another 45 percent goes to higher
education, the Oklahoma School for the Deaf, and the
Oklahoma School for the Blind. The remaining 10 percent
is allocated equally between the Teachers' Retirement
System Dedicated Revenue Revolving Fund and the School
Consolidation and Assistance Fund.[2]

In January, 2007, the $100 million dollar mark was
passed in money raised from the lottery to support common
schools and higher education in Oklahoma. That year Bill
was elected vice chair of the Commission.

"Bill is a good public servant," said longtime friend
Kenneth Brown, "He relates to people in all walks of life.
He is concerned about doing the right thing, of being fair
to everyone. Oklahoma has benefited greatly by Bill's
leadership." [3]

Both Bill and Barbara have served in several capacities
at the University of Oklahoma. In 2004, Bill was elected as a

trustee of the University of Oklahoma Foundation. It has been rewarding for Bill to play even a small part in the miracles that have occurred at OU under the leadership of President David Boren. The assets of the OU Foundation have grown to more than $600 million. OU Vice President for University Development Paul Massad said, "Bill has the unique ability of fully understanding what it takes to complete any and all projects with which he has been involved. It is a trait that only a few people have." [4]

Barbara and Bill and ardent supporters of the University of Oklahoma. Left to right, OU President David L. Boren, Bill, Dean Sul Lee, Barbara, and Jane Harlow. *Courtesy Bill and Barbara Paul.*

Bill and the Paul girls at his induction into the Oklahoma Hall of Fame in 2003.
Left to right, Alison, Bill, Elaine, and Laura. *Courtesy Bill and Barbara Paul.*

Barbara has served as chair of the Board of Visitors of
the Sam Noble Oklahoma Museum of Natural History at OU
and as a member of the Board of Visitors of the College of
Education. Both Barbara and Bill have served a term as chair
of the Bizzell University Library Society. Bill was chair of
the Board of Visitors of the College of Arts and Sciences and
a member of the Board of Visitors of the OU College of Law.

Paul Bell, dean of the OU College of Arts and Sciences,
appreciated service on the Board of Visitors. He said, "Bill is
a very rare breed of alumni. He so loves OU that he would do
anything to help. He is always looking for new opportunities
to help his alma mater." [5]

In 2002, Bill and Barbara made a substantial gift to OU, creating endowments at the College of Law, the College of Arts and Sciences, and the Bizzell Memorial Library. In addition they made grants for current support for the College of Education, the College of Business, and the OU Athletic Deparatment.

Bill became a member of the governing board of Red Earth in 2002. Red Earth is an organization whose mission is to honor and preserve Native American heritage. The group has a museum at the Omniplex in Oklahoma City which includes valuable Native American art and sponsors a nationally-known Native American festival in Oklahoma each year.[6]

Congratulating Bill, left, on his induction into the Oklahoma Hall of Fame are former OU football coach Barry Switzer, George Paul, and Homer Paul. *Courtesy Bill and Barbara Paul.*

In 2003, Bill received the highest honor his native state could bestow upon him—induction into the Oklahoma Hall of Fame, sponsored by the Oklahoma Heritage Association. Bill's Hall of Fame class included Boone Pickens and Robert S. Kerr, Jr.

Bill is excited about the resurgence of the Chickasaw Nation. He is proud of his Native American roots and gives much of the credit for Chickasaw advances to Governor Bill Anoatubby. In 2005, Governor Anoatubby appointed Bill as a director of Bank 2, a bank owned by the Chickasaw Nation. Under the leadership of bank president, Ross Hill, the bank has been successful and is fulfilling a mission of serving and benefiting all Native Americans in the state.[7]

A special room in the OU College of Education is named the Barbara Brite Paul Early Literacy Room. *Courtesy Bill and Barbara Paul.*

Bill's family at the 2003 Oklahoma Hall of Fame ceremony. Left to right, Laura Paul, Steve Paul, George Paul, Barbara Paul, Bill, Elaine Seidel, Homer Paul, Ramona Paul, Alison Miller, and Darren Seidel. *Courtesy Bill and Barbara Paul.*

In 2006, this cartoon drawn by Kevin Stark appeared in the *Pauls Valley Daily Democrat*, calling Bill the "king of Pauls Valley." *Courtesy Bill and Barbara Paul.*

In January, 2006, Bill hunted ducks in Arkansas with his brother, Homer, left, and longtime friend, Jack Middleton, right. Bill's Labrador retriever, Hershey, is at right. *Courtesy Bill and Barbara Paul.*

Others recognize Bill's pride in his Chickasaw heritage. Judge Valerie Couch introduced Bill at an Oklahoma County Bar Association Law Day luncheon in 2001 and said, "To each task, he brings the enthusiasm and curiosity of a child, the intelligence and tenacity of his Chickasaw ancestors, and the grace and good judgment of our wisest elders." [8]

As an example of Bill's pride in his ancestry, he appeared on commercials for the Chickasaw Nation. Bill, astronaut John Herrington, government official Neal McCaleb, Tom Love, and others were featured on the commercials that portrayed the successes and contributions of the modern Chickasaw Nation.

United States District Judge Ralph Thompson paid tribute to Bill's life in the legal profession when Bill was awarded the Justice Marian Opala Award for Lifetime Achievement in Law by Oklahoma City University in 2004. Judge Thompson said, "From a Garvin County dairy farm to a legal leader of the world, this fine man, undisputedly one of America's premier lawyers, is a most deserving and worthy product of Thomas Jefferson's dreamed-of 'democracy of opportunity.'" [9]

Many of Bill's friends and associates believe his childhood in a small town made him a better person. Longtime assistant Joyce Coleson reflected, "He has never left Pauls Valley. He is still a little boy from Pauls Valley in some ways. It amazes him that people think he is something special. His special quality in life comes from his genuine equal treatment of all people—from the waitress who serves him morning coffee to the Queen of England. He is truly no respecter of persons." [10]

Bill has never forgotten his roots. When he was inducted into the Pauls Valley Hall of Fame in 2001, he memorialized the contributions made by his hometown:

I owe this place, this town, its institutions and its people much more than I could ever replay. My values, my beliefs, and all the foundations of my life were formed here. The basic education on which all else was built was given to me here...I thank Pauls Valley for the values it gave me...I have always felt I "belonged" to Pauls Valley, that I was part of the community and part of its history.[11]

Bill and Barbara are avid fans of University of Oklahoma football. At the 2005 Sugar Bowl in New Orleans are, left to right, Billy Bowden, Jane Harlow, Lil Ross, Bill Ross, Ann Workman, Bill, Barbara, and Dick Workman. *Courtesy Bill and Barbara Paul.*

SOME FANTASTIC CO-WORKERS

If I have achieved anything notable in my career, it is due
in large part to the magnificent support of the people who
have worked with me.
—Bill Paul

Since his early days as a lawyer at Crowe & Dunlevy, Bill was fortunate to be surrounded by competent and hard-working people whom he credits with his success in life. Among his assistants at the law firm were Billie Gardner, who worked for Bill for 17 years; Jere Cash, and Linda Leemaster. Shawn Jones was Bill's legal assistant both at Crowe & Dunlevy and later at Phillips Petroleum Company.

At Phillips, Bill's first secretary was Corinne Hutchison who had been a legal secretary to the Phillips' general counsel for many years. She "broke" Bill in at the company. Her wisdom was invaluable because she knew the customs, practices, and procedures of the company and of the legal division. After Bill had been in the position for seven months, Corinne retired, over his strong objection. Corinne said to

Bill, "It is time for me to go, and I think now you are ready to fly on your own." Norma McDonald ably filled Corinne's shoes and was Bill's assistant at Phillips for his remaining ten years.[1]

Bill worked with a great staff during his service to bar associations. There was always strong support for him at the Oklahoma County Bar Association and the Oklahoma Bar Association. Staff meant a great deal to Bill during his year as president-elect and year as president of the American Bar Association. The first job took about two-thirds of his time and the presidency took "150 percent" of his waking hours.

At the ABA, Bill was impressed with the quality of the staff. Robert A. Stein was executive director. He was a former dean of the University of Minnesota College of Law and had both inherited and assembled a great team. Patsy Englehart headed the staff of the Office of the President. That staff included Luke Bierman, "a person of exceptional ability," who worked with Bill on projects and speeches. Other ABA staff members who made Bill's time enjoyable and productive were Marina Jacks, director of the Office of Policy Administration; Mary Cavalini, director of Meetings and Travel; Alpha Brady of the Office of the President; and Robert Evans who ran the ABA office in Washington, D.C.[2]

Joyce Coleson worked for Bill in two capacities. She was assigned as his legal secretary and assistant when he returned to Crowe & Dunlevy in 1996. During the two years he served the ABA, Crowe & Dunlevy and the ABA made it possible for her to work full-time on ABA matters. She was Bill's principal source of support in Oklahoma City. Bill said,

"She did a great job and made many friends throughout the country." After his term as ABA president, Joyce continued her work as Bill's assistant at the law firm until she became administrative assistant to Judge Jerome Holmes when he was appointed to the United States Court of Appeals for the Tenth Circuit in 2006.

Friendships are special to Bill and Barbara Paul. Left to right, Billy Bowden, Jane Harlow, United States Court of Appeals Judge Robert Henry, and Jan Henry. *Courtesy Bill and Barbara Paul.*

Joyce is typical of Bill's former employees who hold him in such high regard. "The first time he corrected me when I did something wrong, I was upset and cried," she said, "but within minutes he was saying, 'That's OK.' He never made me feel small and stupid." [3]

The ability to focus may have helped Bill juggle bar association and law practice obligations. Joyce said, "He's always focused. When he focuses on something, he get's it done. If he is on vacation, he can focus on fun. But when he is in 'work mode,' there is no twiddling of the thumbs. There was always something to be done, and he was focused on it." [4]

Bill frequently told his bar association staff members that they would labor under the 90-10 rule—they would do 90 percent of the work but receive only ten percent of the credit. About the people who have helped him in staff positions along the way, Bill said, "They were absolutely essential to the success of a practicing lawyer and a bar president." [5]

FAMILY

Barbara was and is very well-suited to be a lawyer's wife. She shared my interests and my ambitions and always helped me in my career.
—Bill Paul

Not long after Bill and Mary Lynn were divorced, Bill began dating Barbara Elaine Brite of Norman. After graduating from OU in 1956, she taught kindergarten for four years in Coronado, California. She returned to Norman and had taught second grade in the Norman public school system for three years. She was 27 and had never been married. Bill was divorced with two "wonderful" children, George, age six, and Alison, age three.[1]

After a few months of dating, Bill proposed to Barbara. He first had to convince her that as a divorced man, he could be a good husband. Finally, he succeeded, and they were married at Crown Heights Methodist Church in Oklahoma City on September 27, 1963.

Bill and Barbara began their marriage with no money.
Bill had invested his limited funds in a small house at 1604
Brighton Avenue in The Village, a north Oklahoma City
suburb. However, they had no money for furniture. As a
major commitment to the marriage, Barbara liquidated her
teacher's retirement account in California and used the money
to buy furniture.[2]

While still in high school,
Barbara was crowned as
Belle of the Ball by the OU
Naval ROTC unit. *Courtesy
Bill and Barbara Paul.*

Barbara Brite was a campus
beauty queen while a student at the
University of Oklahoma. *Courtesy Bill
and Barbara Paul.*

Bill escorts daughter, Elaine, at her wedding to Darren Seidel. A photograph of the wedding appeared in Martha Stewart's wedding magazine. *Courtesy Bill and Barbara Paul.*

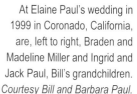

At Elaine Paul's wedding in 1999 in Coronado, California, are, left to right, Braden and Madeline Miller and Ingrid and Jack Paul, Bill's grandchildren. *Courtesy Bill and Barbara Paul.*

From the very beginning, Barbara was "a perfect companion" for Bill's life and career. She helped in recruiting young lawyers by hosting parties in the Paul home. She was understanding about the demands of a law practice and adjusted to a six-day work week with two late evenings as well. She also understood their situation of having little money. Before they were married, Bill explained his obligations to his children, so Barbara was prepared for sparse household budgets.[3]

William Stephen Paul was born January 22, 1971. *Courtesy Bill and Barbara Paul.*

Laura Elaine Paul was born June 1, 1967. *Courtesy Bill and Barbara Paul.*

However, financial matters improved as Bill became established in his practice. In 1966, they bought their first new car and began to treat themselves to an annual shopping spree in Dallas three years later. Bill remembered, "Spending money is a lot of fun if you have gone through a period of years without having any money to spend." [4]

Bill and Barbara have always enjoyed great communication. Bill loves to tell the story of an occasion in the early 1980s when he told Barbara over breakfast that he was taking his very attractive and married secretary, Linda Leemaster, to lunch at the Whitehall Club atop the Fidelity Bank Building. Bill said, "Since you will probably hear about it by 2:00 p.m. this afternoon, I wanted to give you advance notice." It was the third anniversary of Linda's assignment as Bill's secretary. Barbara quietly asked, "Who remembered the anniversary?" [5]

Another favorite story came from the first years Bill was general counsel of Phillips and decided he and Barbara needed to "do some budgeting and save more money." Bill had a difficult time in getting Barbara to sit down and talk about the subject. When finally they did, he began the discussion in his customary way of making a pronouncement. Barbara then said, "Just when were you made king?" Bill thought a moment and said, "Why, it was when I married a queen, my dear!" That response softened Barbara to the budgeting idea.[6]

Bill joins the kitchen crew to help prepare Thanksgiving dinner. *Courtesy Bill and Barbara Paul.*

Bill pours a glass of wine for Barbara at a traditional Paul Thanksgiving feast. *Courtesy Bill and Barbara Paul.*

Barbara and Bill have two children. Laura Elaine Paul was born June 1, 1967, and William Stephen "Steve" Paul was born January 22, 1971. "Barbara has been a wonderful mother and stepmother," Bill bragged. On the stepmother side, George and Alison have spent a lot of time in Bill and Barbara's home, usually in the summer, and Barbara worked hard to see that they had a good time. They often visited Six Flags Over Texas for a long weekend. One summer, before Barbara and Bill had children, George and Alison vacationed with them in California, including Disneyland, while Bill fulfilled his two-week annual Marine Corps Reserve training.[7]

At the 1999 American Bar Association meeting in London are, left to right, Darren Seidel, Barbara Paul, Elaine Paul Seidel, Bill Paul, Laura Paul, and Steve Paul. Courtesy American Bar Association. *Courtesy Bill and Barbara Paul.*

At Temple Church in London, where Bill participated in the Bible reading, are, left to right, Alison Paul Miller, George Paul, Steve Paul, Barbara Paul, and Bill. Courtesy American Bar Association. *Courtesy Bill and Barbara Paul.*

As a mother, Barbara was "incredible." Especially during the early years when Bill was very busy with his law practice, Barbara assumed almost full responsibility of caring for the children. "She appeared to relish the task," Bill said, "She never complained and considered that was her contribution to furthering my legal career." [8]

Family friend, Jane Harlow, observed, "Barbara was a wonderful wife and mother. She was always loyal and there for Bill. She always kept the home fires burning. She even put in a warming drawer, because Bill was often late for dinner." Harlow and Barbara had been friends, and mothers with same-age children, for many years. She was the matron of honor at Bill and Barbara's wedding and Barbara was maid of

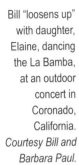

Bill "loosens up" with daughter, Elaine, dancing the La Bamba, at an outdoor concert in Coronado, California. *Courtesy Bill and Barbara Paul.*

honor at Jane's wedding to James "Jim" Harlow.[9]

A great Paul family story had to do with Barbara's stern instructions to Elaine when she was seven years old. One Saturday summer afternoon, Bill was driving home from the office when he spotted Elaine in swimsuit, with towels and swim toys, walking along the sidewalk. Bill stopped and discovered Barbara was allowing Elaine to walk the two blocks to the country club to go swimming. When Bill offered to give his daughter a ride, she said, "No, I can't. Mom said I should never get in a car with any man." Obviously, Barbara had made her point about not getting into a car with strange men.[10]

When it came time for Elaine to attend school, Bill and Barbara had a difference of opinion. Both were products of public schools which had served them well. Bill wanted

Elaine to attend public school. Barbara, who had seven years experience as an early childhood teacher, was impressed with the program at Casady School, an independent college preparatory school founded in 1947, located on an 80-acre campus in north Oklahoma City. Affiliated with the Episcopal Church, Casady has a reputation for academic excellence.[11]

Barbara won the battle and both Elaine and Steve attended Casady. Elaine was a "lifer" at Casady, attending 15 years from pre-school to graduation from the twelfth grade. Steve attended Casady 14 years—he completed his ninth-grade year in Bartlesville. "Barbara was right," Bill reflected, "The Casady experience was terrific for both children."

Both children finished Casady well prepared for college. Elaine finished first in her class and was admitted to every college to which she applied, including Harvard, Princeton, Stanford, and Duke. Steve also did well academically and on graduation received the prestigious Sokolosky Award for outstanding service to the school as a student. Steve was a starter on the volleyball team which was undefeated his senior year. The star of the team was Steve Murphy, son of Bill's law partner, Brooke Smith Murphy.[12]

Some of the best family times were on vacations trips, during spring break or in connection with Bill's military reserve training. Several spring breaks were spent at Padre Island, Texas, where the family rented a condominium on the beach. In 1984, the Pauls bought, along with close friends from New Mexico, a condominium in Maui, in the Kahana Beach area between Kaanipali and Kapalua. They spent several summer trips in Maui.

BELOW: Braden, left, and Madeline Miller, are the children of Alison Paul Miller and Doug Miller. *Courtesy Bill and Barbara Paul.*

ABOVE: Bill's first grandchild was Jack Paul. *Courtesy Bill and Barbara Paul.*

RIGHT: Grandchildren Lauren and Will Seidel are the children of Elaine and Darren Seidel. *Courtesy Bill and Barbara Paul.*

LEFT: William Paul, born in 2006, is the latest Paul grandchild. *Courtesy Bill and Barbara Paul.*

In 1985, the family spent two weeks in Europe, in Great Britain, Germany, Austria, Italy, Switzerland, and France. In 1989, a spectacular two week trip included visits in the Orient to Hong Kong and Thailand.

In 1991, Bill realized a long dream of taking the entire family on a private cruise on a sailing ship in the Caribbean Sea. *The Endless Summer II* sailed under the British flag and cruised in the British Virgin Islands. Bill, Barbara, George and his wife, Karen, Elaine and her boyfriend, and Steve made the voyage. Alison and her husband, Doug, were unable to make the trip.

Grandfather Bill and granddaughter, Ingrid Paul. *Courtesy Bill and Barbara Paul.*

The kitchen is a favorite place for the girls of the Paul household. Left to right, Barbara, Elaine, and Laura. *Courtesy Bill and Barbara Paul.*

One of the most humorous family stories occurred on that vacation. It was August in the Caribbean and quite warm. Elaine's boyfriend chose to sleep on the benches on the main deck of the ship rather than in his cabin. One dark night, Barbara decided it was too warm for her in their cabin and said, "I'm going to go up and sleep on the deck." She was groping her way in the darkness when she suddenly touched Elaine's boyfriend, who exclaimed, "Mrs. Paul!" Barbara was surprised and embarrassed and could only imagine what was going through the young man's mind. The story has given the family many laughs over the years.[13]

Bill and Barbara consider their finest achievement in life making it possible for each of the four children to attend the college or university of his or her choice. Each child has two degrees. The pennants on the wall at the Paul home represent their children's schools. George graduated from Dartmouth College and the Yale School of Law. Alison graduated from Vanderbilt University and Tulane University. Elaine is a graduate of Stanford University and Harvard University. Steve graduated from DePauw University and the University of Oklahoma.[14]

On the graduate school level, George received his law degree at Yale, Alison earned her Masters in Business Administration (MBA) at Tulane, Elaine received her MBA at Harvard, and Steve earned his MBA at OU. Because both Bill and Barbara graduated from OU, they are fond of saying that Steve is the only child who received a quality education.[15]

Bill and Barbara enjoy an outdoor concert in a park in Coronado, California, where they spend several weeks each year. Barbara taught school in Coronado before she met Bill. *Courtesy Bill and Barbara Paul.*

Bill and daughter, Elaine, get ready for a bicycle trip. *Courtesy Bill and Barbara Paul.*

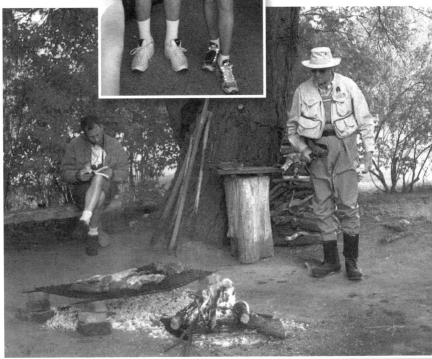

Bill, right, and son, George, trout fishing in Argentina in 2004. *Courtesy Bill and Barbara Paul.*

The Pauls had a unique financial arrangement with each of their children. Bill and Barbara would pay tuition and fees, room and board, buy all books and supplies, and pay transportation to and from school. Each child had to work each summer to earn money for incidental expenses. It was important to Bill and Barbara that the children did not have to work during the school year in order to devote their time and energy to studies and that they finished school without debt. Those objectives were accomplished for all four children.[16]

Bill's oldest son, George, has a distinguished record of academic achievement. He ranked third in the Dartmouth College Class of 1979, with a straight-A average, and was a member of Kappa Kappa Kappa social fraternity. Even though Yale Law School did not award letter grades, George received honors, for students near the top of the class, in every course he took.

George is a successful trial lawyer with the Lewis & Roca firm in Phoenix, Arizona. While still a student in law school, he interned at the firm in the summer of 1981. After graduation a year later, the firm offered him a job as an associate attorney. He has been there since. George loves the outdoors, leads a small group of brave souls on a hike to the bottom of the Grand Canyon each year—Bill accompanied the group in 1998—and enjoys his hobby of bird-watching.[17]

George has become a nationally-recognized expert in the field of electronic discovery, e-discovery, a term familiar to lawyers. He is divorced and shares custody of two children, Jack, born in 1992, and Ingrid, born in 1995. They live in a home at the base of Squaw Peak in Phoenix. When Bill was a

bit younger, he often accompanied George on half-day hikes
to the top of Squaw Peak.

After she completed her bachelor's program at
Vanderbilt, with a fine academic record and as member of
the Chi Omega sorority, Alison worked for a year as a legal
assistant in a Nashville, Tennessee, law firm. She was then
admitted to the MBA program at Tulane and lived in New
Orleans, Louisiana, for two years as a student. Bill and
Barbara enjoyed their visits to Tulane, partly because Alison
knew the best restaurants in New Orleans.[18]

After graduating from Tulane, Alison took her first job
as the deputy administrator of a small, 200-bed hospital
in New Iberia, Louisiana. She gained valuable experience
because, in a small hospital, she had to learn a variety of jobs.
She married Douglas Miller, a graduate of the University
of Michigan and the Tulane University School of Law. He
received his master's degree in taxation from the law school
at New York University. After they were married, Doug
worked as a clerk for one of the judges of the United States
Tax Court.[19]

When Alison and Doug decided it was time to put down
roots, they chose the Pacific Northwest. Neither had been to
that section of the country, but selected Portland, Oregon.
Doug has his own tax law practice and Alison continues to
work as an executive in the healthcare industry, supervising
a staff of about 15 people. They have two children, Braden,
born in 1992, and Madeline, born in 1995. Both children
are bilingual and attend the French American School in
Portland.[20]

Bill, left, and brother, Homer Paul, have maintained a close relationship that began on the dairy farm in Pauls Valley decades ago. *Courtesy Homer Paul.*

During Elaine's senior year at Casady, she and Barbara took a road trip to visit universities to which she had been accepted. She narrowed her choices to Princeton University and Stanford University—she picked the latter. During a weekly telephone conversation in 1985, Elaine announced to her parents, "Mom, Dad, I have decided I am going to stay out here." She has been in California ever since. Elaine was a member of Kappa Kappa Gamma social sorority and graduated with honors.[21]

When Elaine finished Stanford in 1989, she had several job opportunities. She chose the Walt Disney Company that had heavily recruited her. The morning after she accepted the Disney job, she opened her door to her suite in Stanford housing and was greeted by a four-feet-high stuffed Mickey Mouse holding a bottle of champagne in folded arms. Attached to the bottle was a note, "Welcome to the family, Elaine!" Elaine still works for the company and loves her job.[22]

After three years, Elaine left Disney to attend Harvard Business School to earn her MBA. There was no obligation for Disney to rehire her, but the company did, and paid her a "signup bonus" to partially defray the expenses of the two years at Harvard. Because Bill and Barbara had financed the Harvard years, they laid "claim" on the bonus, without success. Bill said, "Elaine had learned her business lessons well at Harvard." [23]

Elaine is now a senior vice president at Disney, working at corporate headquarters in Burbank, California. She is married to Darren Seidel, a business executive who attended San Diego University and earned his MBA at Notre Dame University. Darren also works at Disney. Elaine and Darren have two children, Will, born in 2003, and Lauren, born in 2005. Elaine and Darren travel internationally in their jobs but try to work out their schedules so they are not both out of the country at the same time. [24]

Bill with a Labrador retriever puppy, Hershey, who quickly became a member of the Paul family. *Courtesy Bill and Barbara Paul.*

The youngest Paul child, Steve, was a popular and excellent student at Casady School when he transferred in the ninth grade to Bartlesville public schools because his father had taken the job as general counsel for Phillips Petroleum Company. To make the move, his parents promised that if he was unhappy, he could return to Casady for his final years of high school. Predictably, Steve began marking off the days until he could return.[25]

At the time, Bill's mother lived in the vicinity of Casady School. She offered to "take Steve in" and Steve loved it. He lived with her for three years until he finished high school. Barbara spent about one-third of her time in Oklahoma City. During those visits, Steve lived with her at the Paul home in Quail Creek.[26]

Bill shows off a sailfish caught in the Pacific Ocean in 2004 off the coast of Cabo San Lucas, Mexcio. *Courtesy Rod Matthews.*

ABOVE: Bill with friends, United States District Judge Ralph G. Thompson, left, and Bill Ross, right. *Courtesy Bill and Barbara Paul.*

RIGHT: Bill and Barbara celebrate another happy occasion. *Courtesy Bill and Barbara Paul.*

Steve attended college at DePauw University in Greencastle, Indiana. He chose the school partly because several students from Casady had attended the school. He was a member of the Beta Theta Pi fraternity. Interested in business, he majored in economics at DePauw. After graduating in 1993, he worked in retail stores in Oklahoma City for three years before being admitted to the OU MBA program. He had a high interest in hunting and fishing and was "at home" working in a sporting goods store. He received his MBA in 1998.[27]

After completing the MBA program, Steve took a job with Conoco in Ponca City, Oklahoma. When the company merged with Phillips, Steve moved to Bartlesville where he is a senior analyst in the finance group of the company.

In 2003, Steve married his MBA classmate, Laura McMahon. Laura, a twin, the youngest of 11 children, attended undergraduate school at Oklahoma State University. They have a son, William, born in 2006.

In 2002, Steve, Bill, and Barbara bought an 1,800-acre ranch in Osage County, Oklahoma, about 20 miles northwest of Bartlesville. It is called the Triple P Ranch. Steve manages the ranch and loves to hunt deer and turkey. He has made improvements, built new fences, and upgraded the lakes and ponds. Until 2007 they leased or rented the grassland to cattle operators. Now, the family is in the cattle ranching business in partnership with their neighbor, Kent Trentman, who manages the operation.[28]

Any story of the Paul family must include a reference to another member of the family—Hershey, their female chocolate Labrador retriever. Hershey came to live with the Pauls in 2004—her litter mate, a male black Labrador retriever named Sam, is owned by Steve.

"Volumes could be written about Hershey," Bill said.
She has unbelievably strong retrieving and hunting instincts.
Because Bill takes her hunting infrequently, Hershey has
developed ways of using her instincts in the home. She brings
Bill and Barbara tubes of toothpaste, laundry—she prefers it
before it is washed, important pieces of mail, books, and her
personal chew toys. Barbara said, "She did a great job on the
outdoor furniture, but we love her anyway—and she loves us." [29]

Bill relaxing at the cabin owned by family friend Jane Harlow. *Courtesy Bill and Barbara Paul.*

BIBLIOGRAPHY & SUGGESTED READING

NEWSPAPERS AND PERIODICALS

ABA Journal
Chicago, Illinois

Oklahoma City Times
Oklahoma City, Oklahoma

Oklahoma Journal
Midwest City, Oklahoma

Pauls Valley Daily Democrat
Pauls Valley, Oklahoma

Pauls Valley Enterprise
Pauls Valley, Oklahoma

Sooner Magazine
Norman, Oklahoma

The Chickasaw Chieftan
Ardmore, Oklahoma

The Daily Oklahoman
Oklahoma City, Oklahoma

The Valley News
Pauls Valley, Oklahoma

Tulsa World
Tulsa, Oklahoma

BOOKS

Baird, W. David, and Danney Goble. *The Story of Oklahoma*. Norman:
University of Oklahoma Press, 1994.

Blackburn, Bob L. *Heart of the Promised Land, Oklahoma County: An
Illustrated History*. Woodland Hills, California: Windsor Publications, 1982.

Burke, Bob. *Good Guys Wear White Hats: The Life of George Nigh*. Oklahoma
City: Oklahoma Heritage Association, 2000.

Burke, Bob and Louise Painter. *Justice Served: The Life of Alma Bell Wilson*.
Oklahoma City, Oklahoma Heritage Association, 2001.

Fischer, LeRoy H., editor, *Oklahoma's Governors, 1929-1955*. Oklahoma City:
Oklahoma Historical Society, 1983.

Hazlitt, J.M. *From Bluestem to Golden Trend: A short story of Smith Paul's
Valley*. Pauls Valley, Oklahoma: privately printed, 1956.

Hendrickson, Kenneth E. Jr., editor. *Hard Times in Oklahoma*. Oklahoma City
Oklahoma Historical Society, 1983.

Lambert, Paul F. and Bob L. Blackburn. *"You Know We Belong to the Land:"
The Centennial History of Oklahoma*. Oklahoma City: Oklahoma Heritage
Association, 2007.

Paul, Bill and Cindy Paul. *Shadow of an Indian Star.* Austin, Texas: Synergy
Books, 2005.

Walker, J.R., *A History of Pauls Valley*, unpublished dissertation,
University of Oklahoma, 1953.

BILL PAUL'S FAVORITE QUOTATIONS

ON LIVING

People are not afraid of dying. They are afraid of never having lived.
— Rabbi Harold Kushner

The Moving Finger writes, and having writ moves on; nor all your Piety nor Wit shall lure it back to cancel half a line.
— Omar Khayyam

ON LOVING

If I had never met Marciarose, I would have spent the rest of my life looking for her.
— Jerome Shestack, past president of the American Bar Association, Philadelphia, Pennsylvania, about his wife

ON POLITICS

Some advice I received when running for president of the American Bar Association: You should be for progress, but you should be against change.
— Morris Harrell, past president of the American Bar Association, Dallas, Texas

ON CIVIC SERVICE

My fellow Americans; Ask not what your country can do for you, ask what you can do for your country.
— President John F. Kennedy in his inaugural address, January 20, 1961.

BILL PAUL'S FAVORITE QUOTATIONS

ON HEROISM

Never in the field of human conflict was so much owed by so many to so few.
— Prime Minister Winston Churchill, August 20, 1940, during the Battle of Britain, speaking of Royal Air Force fighter pilots

Uncommon valor was a common virtue.
— Fleet Admiral Chester W. Nimitz, March 16, 1945, speaking of the United States Marines in the battle for Iwo Jima.

ON LEGAL ETHICS

A lawyer should never do anything which he or she would not want to see published on the front page of tomorrow's edition of the daily paper.
— Raymond Tolbert – 1958

The goal of our profession should be to attain the grandeur of its pretensions.
— Ralph Nader – 1989

What we expect of the English barrister is to present the client's case as it is; not as the client might wish it to be.
— Lord Justice Scott Baker of the United Kingdom – 2005

THE OFFICIAL RECORD OF BILL PAUL'S LIFE

PERSONAL INFORMATION

• EDUCATION: University of Oklahoma, B.A. Degree (1952); College of Law, University of Oklahoma, LL.B. Degree (1956); attended Public Schools in Pauls Valley, Oklahoma, graduating from High School in 1948 (Valedictorian)

• DATE AND PLACE OF BIRTH: November 25, 1930 in Pauls Valley, Oklahoma

Professional Career Positions

• CURRENTLY: Of Counsel, Crowe & Dunlevy law firm of Oklahoma City (since January 1, 2005); Co-Chair, Alternative Dispute Resolution Section

• FORMERLY: Senior Vice President and General Counsel of Phillips Petroleum Company from January 1, 1985 until December 31, 1995; Member of Crowe & Dunlevy law firm of Oklahoma City from 1957 until December 31, 1984; Chairman of the firm's Executive Committee (1974-1979); Advisory Directory, January 1, 1996 until December 31, 2004.

PROFESSIONAL ACTIVITIES

AMERICAN BAR ASSOCIATION (ABA)
LEADERSHIP POSITIONS

• President, American Bar Association (1999-2000)

• Member, ABA Board of Governors (1995-2001); Member, Program and Planning Committee

• State Delegate from Oklahoma and Member, ABA Nominating Committee (1986-1995)

• Member, ABA House of Delegates (1975-1977 and 1979-___)

• Chair, Committee on Research About the Future of The Legal Profession (1995-1997)

• Chair, ABA Coalition for Justice (1992-1993)

• Chair, House of Delegates Committee on Ancillary Business (1992-1994)

• Member, House of Delegates Committee on Rules and Calendar (1994-1995)

• ABA Commission on Women in the Profession (1993-95): Vice-Chair (1994-1995)

• ABA Section of Legal Education and Admissions to the Bar: Member, Commission to Review the Substance and Process of ABA's Accreditation of American Law Schools (1994-1995)

• ABA Litigation Section: Member of Council (1990-1993); Co-Chair Committee on Energy Law (1988-1990)

• ABA Business Law Section: Member of Corporate General Counsel Committee (1987-___); Chair of Environmental Law Sub-Committee (1989-1995)

• Charter Member, ABA Special Coordinating Committee on Professionalism (1986-1992)

• Member, ABA Standing Committee on Bar Activities and Services (1983-1986)

• Founder, ABA Legal Opportunity Scholarship Fund for Law Students who are Members of Racial and Ethnic Minorities (1999)

• As ABA President, Established the Latin America Law Initiatives Council and the Africa Law Initiatives Council (1999)

• Chair, ABA Advisory Council on Diversity in the Profession (2000 - 2001)

• Charter Member, ABA Committee on Public Interest Practice (1974 -1980)

• Charter Member, ABA Latin America Law Initiatives Council (1999 - 2005)

• Member, Council, ABA Fund for Justice and Education (1989-94)

STATE AND LOCAL BAR LEADERSHIP POSITIONS

• President, National Conference of Bar Presidents (1986); Member of Executive Council (1978-1987)

• President, Oklahoma Bar Association (1976); Member, Board of Governors (1975-1977)

• President, Oklahoma County Bar Association (1971); Treasurer (1964); Director (1966-1972)

• President, Oklahoma Bar Professional Liability Insurance Company (1976-1984)

• President, Oklahoma County Young Lawyers (1964-1965)

OTHER PROFESSIONAL AND BUSINESS ACTIVITIES

• American College of Trial Lawyers: Fellow, (elected 1978); State Chair for Oklahoma (1985-1987); Member, State Committee (1981-1988)

• American Bar Endowment: President (1997-1998); Member, Board of Directors (1986-2000); Director Emeritus (2000-2005)

• Fellows of American Bar Foundation (elected 1976): Chairman (1990-1991); Life Patron Fellow; Oklahoma State Chair (1982-1984)

• American Bar Foundation: Member, Board of Directors (1988-1991 and 1997-2000)

• Member, Executive Committee, CPR Institute for Dispute Resolution (1992-2000)

• General Committee on Law, American Petroleum Institute (1985-1995); Chairman (1994-1995)

• The Center for American & International Law: Trustee (1982-2005); Vice Chair, Board of Trustees (1995-2005); Chairman, Research Fellows (1992-1993); Trustee Emeritus (2006 -___)

• Member, Association of General Counsel (1989-___)

• Trustee, University of Oklahoma Foundation, Inc. (2003-___)

• Trustee, National Constitution Center, Philadelphia (2001-___)

• Director, National Center for State Courts, Williamsburg, VA (1993-1999); Inducted into the Warren Burger Society (2001)

• Charter Member, Martindale-Hubbell and Lexis-Nexis Advisory Board, New Providence, NJ (1990-___)

• Trustee, American Inns of Court, Arlington, VA (2000-2003)

• Director, American Judicature Society (2001- 05) and (1982-1988); Advisory Board (2006 -___)

• Trustee, Oklahoma Lottery Commission (2005-___); Vice Chairman (2007); Chairman (2008-___)

• Trustee, American Bar Association Museum of Law (2006-___)

• Director and Secretary, American Bar Insurance Corporation (2005-___)

• Director, Liberty National Bank, Banks of Mid-America and Bank One Oklahoma (1976-1997)

• Director, Bank2, Oklahoma City (2005-___)

• Adjunct Professor of Law, Oklahoma City University (1964-1965)

EDUCATION

UNIVERSITY OF OKLAHOMA (UNDERGRADUATE) - B.A. DEGREE, 1952

• Recipient of Gold Letzseiser Medal, awarded annually to the outstanding male graduate (1952)

• Phi Beta Kappa (1952)

• Member, University of Oklahoma Varsity Debate Team (1949-1951)

• Student Commander, NROTC Battalion (1951-1952)

• Scored Highest Marks on Entrance Examination in History of University (1948)

• Winner Pe-et Award as Outstanding Male Freshman Student (1949)

• Outstanding NROTC Student in each of Four Undergraduate Years (1949-1952)

• Winner, First Place Navigation Event in National Intercollegiate Flying Association Competition (1951)

• President, Pe-et Society (Top Ten Junior Male Students) (1951-1952)

• President, Scabbard and Blade Society Class (1951)

• Secretary, Phi Gamma Delta Fraternity (1949-1950); President of Pledge Class (1949)

• Winner, Rotary Award as Outstanding Graduate in Class of '52

• President, Freshman "Y" (1948-1949)

• Inducted in Delta Sigma Rho, Honorary Forensic Society (1950)

• Winner, First Place, Annual Gordon Fuller Oratorical Competition (1950)

UNIVERSITY OF OKLAHOMA (LAW)- LL.B. DEGREE, 1956

• Callahan Company Award for attaining the highest grade average in the Junior Class (1955)

• Order of the Coif (Top 10% of Graduating Class) (1956)

• Winner Moot Court Competition (1955)

• Board of Editors, *Oklahoma Law Review* (1955-1956); Article and Book Review Editor

• Research Assistant to the Dean of the College of Law (1955-1956)

LECTURES AND PUBLICATIONS

• Lecturer - University of Washington College of Law, "Lawyers Serving Society in the New Millennium" (2000)

• Delivered Annual Irving R. Segal Lecture at University of Pennsylvania College of Law, "A Profession for the New Millennium" (2000)

• Delivered Annual Gunderson Lecture at University of South Dakota College of Law; "Recognizing Our Heritage - Diversity and the Native American Lawyer" (2000)

• Delivered Annual C.J. Silas Lecture on Ethics and Leadership at Georgia Institute of Technology, "Ethics in Law and Business: Gone With the Wind or Alive and Well?" (2001)

• Delivered The Annual Minter Lecture in American Business Practice at Oklahoma Baptist University, "Is a Church a Business? - The Separate Worlds of Religion and Finance" (2003)

• Commencement Speaker, University of Oklahoma College of Law, May, 1998

• Commencement Speaker, Oklahoma City University College of Law, May, 1999

• William G. Paul, Remarks of the Outgoing President of the American Bar Association, 31 N.M. L Rev. 55 (2001).

• William G. Paul, Law Day 2001: Home of the Brave. 26 Okla. City U. L. Rev. 1103(2001)

CIVIC ACTIVITIES AND HONORS

• Recipient, Distinguished Service Citation, University of Oklahoma (highest honor conferred by the University), (May 1985)

• Recipient, Honorary Doctor of Laws Degree, Oklahoma City University, (highest honor conferred by the University), (May 1999)

• Oklahoma Hall of Fame Inductee (2003)

• Chickasaw Nation Hall of Fame Inductee (2002)

• Recipient, Distinguished Alumni Award, University of Oklahoma College of Arts and Sciences and the Friends of the College of Arts and Sciences, (1999)

• Lifetime Achievement Award, Oklahoma Bar Association (2000)

• Recipient, 1994 President's Award, Oklahoma Bar Association

• Honorary Bencher, Middle Temple Inn, London (2000)

• Honorary Barrister, Bar of England and Wales (2000)

• Honorary Solicitor, The Law Society of England and Wales (2000)

• Recipient, Justice Marian Opala Award for Lifetime Achievement in Law by Oklahoma City University (2004)

• Inducted into "The Warren E. Burger Society" by National Center for State Courts (2001)   .

• Inducted into "University of Oklahoma Alumni Hall of Fame" (1979)

• Recipient, University of Oklahoma Regents' Alumni Award (1997)

• President, University of Oklahoma Alumni Association (1973)

• Chair, Board of Visitors, University of Oklahoma College of Arts & Sciences (1997-1998)

• President, OU Club of Oklahoma City (1970)

• Chair, Board of Visitors, University of Oklahoma College of Law (1976-1980) and Member, (2000-___)

• President, Bizzell Memorial Library Society, University of Oklahoma (2002-2004)

• American Inns of Court A. Sherman Christensen Award (2006)

• First Recipient of Oklahoma Bar Association Joe Stamper Distinguished Service Award (2003)

• First Recipient of Oklahoma Bar Association William G. Paul Legal Services Award (2005)

• Member, Board of Visitors, University of Oklahoma College of Business (1987-1990)

• Recipient, Eugene Kuntz Award for Leadership in Natural Resources Law and Policy (1994)

• Member, Board of Directors, Oklahoma Arts Institute (1987-1996)

• Member, Board of Directors, Gilcrease Museum, Tulsa (1992-1995)

• Inducted into Pauls Valley Hall of Fame (2001)

• Director, Oklahoma City Chamber of Commerce (1983-1985)

• Member, Executive Committee, Oklahoma City United Way (1980-1984); Chair, Lawyers Division Oklahoma City United Way (1980)

• Director, Red Earth, Inc. (2000-___): Vice President (2006-___)

• Member, Oklahoma Judicial Evaluation (Blue Ribbon) Commission (1998-1999)

• Named the Outstanding Young Oklahoman by Oklahoma Jaycees (1965); Outstanding Young Man of Oklahoma City (1965)

• Recipient, ABA Spirit of Excellence Award for Commitment to Diversity in the Legal Profession (2002)

MILITARY SERVICE AND HONORS

• Colonel, U.S. Marine Corps (active duty 1952-1954, including Korean service), and U.S. Marine Corps Reserve (1954-75)

• Guest of Honor, United States Marine Corps Evening Parade, Washington, DC (2000)

CHURCH

Member, Westminster Presbyterian Church, Oklahoma City (1996-___); First Presbyterian Church, Bartlesville (1985-1995), Trustee and Treasurer; Covenant Presbyterian Church, Oklahoma City (1973-1984); First Presbyterian Church, Oklahoma City (1964-1972), Deacon; First Presbyterian Church, Norman (1953-1963), Deacon and Trustee; and First Methodist Church, Pauls Valley (1930-1952)

FAMILY

WIFE: Married to Barbara Brite Paul of Norman, Oklahoma

CHILDREN: Four children, two sons and two daughters: George L. Paul, graduate of Dartmouth (1979) and Yale Law School (1982), of Phoenix, Arizona; Alison Paul Miller, graduate of Vanderbilt (1982) and MBA graduate of Tulane (1985), of Portland, Oregon; Elaine Paul Seidel, graduate of Stanford (1989) and MBA graduate of Harvard Business School (1994) of Los Angeles, California; and Steve Paul, graduate of DePauw University, Greencastle, Indiana (1993) and MBA graduate of Michael F. Price College of Business, University of Oklahoma (1998) of Tulsa, Oklahoma.

NOTES

Chapter One
PIONEER HERITAGE

1. www.tolatsga.org

2. www.chickasaw.net, the official website of the Chickasaw Nation; mshistory.k12.ms.us

3. *Pauls Valley Daily Democrat* (Pauls Valley, Oklahoma), July 29, 1984.

4. Transcript of memoirs of William G. Paul hereafter referred to as Bill Paul memoirs, Oklahoma Heritage Association archives Oklahoma City, Oklahoma, hereafter referred to as Heritage Archives.

5. Ibid.

6. Ibid.

7. *Pauls Valley Daily Democrat*, July 29, 1984.

8. Ibid.

9. Ibid.

10. Ellen Hayhurst, *The Old Cemetery*, May 26, 1969, college history project.

11. *Pauls Valley Daily Democrat*, July 29, 1984.

12. Ibid.

13. Ibid.

14. Ibid.

15. J.M. Hazlitt, *From Bluestem to Golden Trend: A short Story of Smith Paul's Valley*, privately printed, 1956.

16. Bill Paul memoirs.

17. The intriguing story of the Paul family is told in a historical fiction setting, *Shadow of an Indian Star*, by Bill and Cindy Paul (Austin, Texas: Synergy Books, 2005), hereafter referred to as *Shadow of an Indian Star*. The co-author of the book is a distant cousin to the subject of this biography.

18. Bill Paul memoirs.

19. Ibid.

20. *Shadow of an Indian Star*, p. 398.

21. *The Chickasaw Chieftan* (Ardmore, Oklahoma), October 22, 1891.

22. *Shadow of an Indian Star*

Chapter Two
LIFE ON THE FARM

1. Interview with Victoria Rosser Paul, September 14, 1937, Indian Pioneer Papers, Oklahoma Historical Society, Oklahoma City, Oklahoma.

2. Ibid.

3. Bob Burke and Louise Painter, *Justice Served: The Life of Alma Bell Wilson* (Oklahoma City: Oklahoma Heritage Association, 2001), p. 14.

4. *The Valley News* (Pauls Valley, Oklahoma), December 22, 1898.

5. Interview with Winona James Gunning, known as "Aunt Jim" to the Paul family, July 20, 2004, hereafter referred to as Winona James Gunning interview.

6. *Pauls Valley Enterprise* (Pauls Valley, Oklahoma), September 25, 1930.

7. Bill Paul memoirs.

8. Bill Paul Chickasaw Multimedia interview, 2005, hereafter referred to as Bill Paul Chickasaw Multimedia interview.

9. Bill Paul memoirs.

10. Ibid.

11. Ibid.

12. *Justice Served*, p. 29.

13. LeRoy H. Fischer, editor, *Oklahoma's Governors, 1929-1955* (Oklahoma City: Oklahoma Historical Society, 1983), p. 8.

14. Ibid., p. 6-7.

15. Ibid., p. 10.

16. Kenneth E. Hendrickson, Jr., editor, *Hard Times in Oklahoma* (Oklahoma City: Oklahoma Historical Society, 1983), p. 131.

17. *Oklahoma's Governors, 1929-1955*, p. 11.

18. Bill Paul memoirs.

19. Ibid.

20. Ibid.

21. *Justice Served*, p. 30.

22. Bill Paul memoirs.

23. Quoted in J. R. Walker, *A History of Pauls Valley*, dissertation, University of Oklahoma, 1953.

24. Bill Paul memoirs.

25. Interview with Winona James Gunning, July 20, 2004, hereafter referred to as Winona James Gunning interview.

26. Interview with Homer Paul, Jr., May 20, 2005, hereafter referred to as Homer Paul, Jr. interview.

27. Bill Paul memoirs.

28. Homer Paul, Jr. interview.

29. Bill Paul memoirs.

30. Ibid.

31. Ibid.

32. Ibid.

33. Ibid.

Chapter Three
GROWING INTO A MAN

1. Winona James Gunning interview.

2. Ibid.

3. Homer Paul, Jr. interview.

4. Winona James Gunning interview

5. Ibid.

6. Homer Paul, Jr. interview.

7. Bill Paul Chickasaw Multimedia interview.

8. Interview with Robert D. Fields, August 4, 2005, hereafter referred to as Robert D. Fields interview.

9. Letter from Nadine Holloway to Bob Burke, June 29, 2005.

10. Letter from Lou Lindsey Hall, June 20, 2005.

11. Bill Paul memoirs.

12. Letter from William J. Robinson to Bob Burke, March 30, 2005.

13. Bill Paul memoirs.

14. Robert D. Fields interview.

15. Bill Paul memoirs.

16. Ibid.

17. Ibid.

18. Ibid.

19. Ibid.

20. Robert D. Fields interview.

21. Bill Paul memoirs.

22. Ibid.

23. Ibid.

24. Ibid.

25. Ibid.

26. Ibid.

27. Ibid.

Chapter Four
COLLEGE AND FAMILY CRISIS

1. Bill Paul memoirs.

2. Ibid.

3. Ibid.

4. Interview with Don Symcox, April 11, 2005.

5. Bill Paul memoirs.

6. Ibid.

7. Winona James Gunning interview.

8. Homer Paul, Jr. interview.

9. Bill Paul memoirs.

10. "The President Speaks," *Sooner Magazine* (Norman, Oklahoma), September, 1949.

11. Bill Paul memoirs.

12. Interview with DeVier Pierson, July 2, 2005, hereafter referred to as DeVier Pierson interview.

13. Ibid.

14. Bill Paul memoirs.

15. Ibid.

16. Interview with E. Deane Kanaly, June 8, 2005.

17. Bill Paul memoirs.

18. Ibid.

19. Ibid.

20. Ibid.

Chapter Five
FLYING AND CRUISING

1. Bill Paul memoirs.

2. Ibid.

3. Ibid.

4. Interview with Lee West, April 7, 2005.

5. Bill Paul memoirs.

6. Ibid.

7. *Justice Served*, p. 45, quoting historian Freda Diane Deskin.

8. Bill Paul memoirs.

9. Ibid.

10. Ibid.

11. Ibid.

Chapter Six
ESPRIT de CORPS

1. Bill Paul memoirs.

2. Ibid.

3. Ibid.

4. Ibid.

5. Ibid.

6. Ibid.

7. Ibid.

8. Ibid.

9. Ibid.

10. Ibid.

11. Ibid.

12. Ibid.

13. Ibid.

14. Ibid.

15. Ibid.

16. Ibid.

17. Ibid.

18. Ibid.

Chapter Seven
KOREA

1. Bill Paul memoirs.

2. Ibid.

3. Ibid.

4. Ibid.

5. Ibid.

6. Ibid.

7. Ibid.

8. Ibid.

9. Ibid.

10. Ibid.

11. Ibid.

12. Ibid.

Chapter Eight
RETURN TO LAW SCHOOL

1. Bill Paul memoirs.

2. Ibid.

3. Bill Paul memoirs; Lee West interview.

4. Ibid.

5. Homer Paul, Jr. interview.

6. Lee West interview.

7. Bill Paul memoirs.

8. Ibid.

9. Ibid.

Chapter Nine
FLEDGING LAWYER

1. Bill Paul memoirs.

2. Ibid.

3. Ibid.

4. www.crowedunlevy.com, the official website of Crowe & Dunlevy, P.C.

5. Ibid.

6. Ibid.

7. Ibid; Bill Paul memoirs.

8. Bill Paul memoirs.

9. Ibid.

10. Ibid.

11. Ibid.

12. Ibid.

13. Ibid.

14. Ibid.

15. Ibid.

16. Ibid.

17. Ibid.

18. Ibid.

19. Ibid.

20. Ibid.

21. Ibid.

22. *Prudential Ins. v. Prudential Life and Cas. Ins.*, 1962 OK 184, 377 P.2d. 556 (Oklahoma Supreme Court, 1962).

23. Bill Paul memoirs.

Chapter Ten
ON THE JOB TRAINING

1. Interview with William J. Holloway, Jr., April 6, 2005, hereafter referred to as William J. Holloway, Jr. interview.

2. Bill Paul memoirs.

3. William J. Holloway, Jr. interview.

4. Interview with Bruce H. Johnson, January 31, 2005.

5. Bill Paul memoirs.

6. Ibid.

7. Ibid.

8. Ibid.

9. Ibid.

10. Ibid.

11. Ibid.

12. Ibid.

13. Ibid.

14. Ibid.

15. Ibid.

16. Bill Paul memoirs.

17. Ibid.

18. See *State ex rel. Nesbitt v. Apco Oil Corp.*, 1977 OK 144, 569 P.2d 434.

19. Bill Paul memoirs.

20. Ibid.

21. Ibid.

22. Ibid.

Chapter Eleven
BUILDING AN INSTITUTION

1. Interview with Andy Coats, June 15, 2007, hereafter referred to as Andy Coats interview.

2. Bill Paul memoirs.

3. Ibid.

4. Andy Coats interview.

5. Bill Paul memoirs.

6. Ibid.

7. Ibid.

8. Ibid.

9. Ibid.

10. William J. Holloway, Jr. interview.

11. Andy Coats interview.

12. Bill Paul memoirs.

13. Ibid.

14. Ibid.

15. Ibid.

16. Ibid.

17. Ibid.

18. Ibid.

19. Bruce Johnson interview.

20. Bill Paul memoirs.

21. Ibid..

22. Ibid.

23. Ibid.

24. Ibid.

25. Ibid.

Chapter Twelve
FOUR SEASONS

1. Bill Paul memoirs

2. Ibid.

3. I bid.

4. Ibid. See *Arthur Andersen & Co. v. State of Ohio*, 502 F.2d 834 (1974); cert. denied 419 U.S. 1034, 95 S.Ct. 516 (1974). See also *Arthur Andersen & Co. vs. Bank of America*, 493 F.2d 1288 (1974; *Schwenienger v. Ralston & Co.*, 63 F.R.D. 598 (1973).

5. Bill Paul memoirs.

6. Ibid.

Chapter Thirteen
CITY OF FAITH

1. www.en.wikipedia. org/wikiOral_Roberts

2. Bill Paul memoirs.

3. Ibid.

4. Ibid.

5. Ibid.

6. Ibid.

7. Ibid.

8. Ibid.

9. Ibid.

10. Ibid.

11. Ibid.

12. *Tulsa Area Hospital Council, Inc. v. Oral Roberts University*, 1981 OK 29, 626 P.2d 316 (Okla. 1981)

13. Ibid.

Chapter Fourteen
SILKWOOD

1. Bill Paul memoirs.

2. Ibid.

3. Ibid.

4. Ibid.

5. See *The Killing of Karen Silkwood*, by Richard Rashke, Houghton Mifflin Company, 1981.

6. Bill Paul memoirs.

7. Ibid.

8. *The Daily Oklahoman*, November 6, 1976.

9. Ibid.

10. Bill Paul memoirs.

11. Ibid.

12. 460 F.Supp. 399 (1978)

13. 637 F.2d 743 (1980)

14. Bill Paul memoirs.

15. 563 F.2d 433 (1977)

16. Bill Paul memoirs.

17. Ibid.

18. Ibid.

19. www.en.wikipedia org/wiki/Karen Silkwood.

20. Bill Paul memoirs.

21. Ibid.

22. Ibid.

Chapter Fifteen
A MEDIA CIRCUS

1. www.spencelawyers com, the official Web site of Gerry Spence's law firm.

2. Bill Paul memoirs.

3. Ibid.

4. Ibid.

5. Ibid.

6. Ibid.

7. Ibid.

8. Ibid.

9. Ibid.

10. Ibid.

11. www.threemiileisland org

12. Ibid., www. en.wikipedia.org/wiki/ Three_Mile_Island

13. *The Daily Oklahoman*, May 15, 1979.

14. Ibid.

15. Ibid., December 16, 1999.

16. Bill Paul memoirs.

17. Ibid.

18. 485 F.Supp. 566 (1979)

19. Bill Paul memoirs.

20. *The Daily Oklahoman*, November 18, 1980.

21. Ibid.

22. 667 F.2d 908 (1982)

23. 464 U.S. 238 (1984)

24. 769 F.2d 1451 (1985)

25. Bill Paul memoirs.

Chapter Sixteen
GENERAL COUNSEL

1. Bill Paul memoirs.

2. www.conocophillips com, the official Web site of ConocoPhillips.

3. Bill Paul memoirs.

4. Ibid.

5. Ibid.

6. Ibid.

7. Ibid.

8. Interview with C.J. "Pete" Silas, November 15, 2005, Heritage Archives.

9. *The Daily Okalhoman*, November 7, 1984.

10. Bill Paul memoirs.

11. Ibid.

12. Ibid.

13. www.en.wikipedia org/wiki/Boone Pickens

14. Ibid.

15. Bill Paul memoirs.

16. Letter from John L. Williford to Eric Dabney, May 12, 2005, hereafter referred to as John L. Williford letter.

17. Bill Paul memoirs.

18. Ibid.

19. Ibid.

20. Ibid.

21. Ibid.

22. Ibid.

23. Ibid.

24. Ibid.

25. Ibid.

26. Ibid.

27. Ibid.

Chapter Seventeen
CORPORATE LEGAL HURDLES

1. Bill Paul Memoirs.

2. Ibid.

3. Ibid.

4. Ibid.

5. Ibid.

6. Ibid.

7. Ibid.

8. Ibid.

9. John L. Williford letter.

10. Bill Paul memoirs.

11. Ibid.

12. Interview with Bake Tartt, January 15, 2006, hereafter referred to as Blake Tartt interview.

13. John L. Williford letter.

14. Bill Paul memoirs.

15. Ibid.

16. Ibid.

Chapter Eighteen
SERVICE TO THE BAR

1. Bill Paul memoirs.

2. Ibid.

3. Ibid.

4. Ibid.

5. Ibid.

6. Ibid.

7. Ibid.

8. www.abanet.org., the official Website of the American Bar Association.

9. Bill Paul memoirs.

10. Interview with Jack Middleton, January 15, 2006.

11. Interview with Stell Huie, march 5, 2006.

12. Bill Paul memoirs.

13. Letter from James Sturdivant to Eric Dabney, March 14, 2005, hereafter referred to as James Sturdivant letter.

14. Interview with Will Hoch, April 1, 2005, hereafter referred to as Will Hoch interview.

15. Interview with Bill Ross, April 14, 2005.

16. Bill Paul memoirs.

17. Ibid.

18. Ibid.

19. Ibid.

20. Will Hoch interview.

21. Bill Paul memoirs.

22. Excerpts of "President's Message," from issues of the *ABA Journal*, published by the American Bar Association, Chicago, Illinois, hereafter referred to as *ABA Journal* exerpts.

Chapter Nineteen
MAKE THE PROFESSION BETTER

1. *ABA Journal* excerpts.

2. Bill Paul memoirs.

3. *ABA Journal* excerpts.

4. Bill Paul memoirs.

5. Ibid.

6. Ibid.

7. Ibid.

8. Ibid.

9. Ibid.

10. Ibid.

11. Ibid.

12. Ibid.

13. Ibid.

14. Ibid.

15. James Sturdivant letter.

16. Bill Paul memoirs.

17. Ibid.

18. Ibid.

19. *ABA Journal* excerpts.

Chapter Twenty
COMMUNITY SERVICE

1. Bill Paul memoirs.

2. www.lottery.ok.gov,
the official Website
of the Oklahoma Lottery
Commission.

3. Interview with Kenneth
Brown, March 22, 2006.

4. Letter from Paul Massad
to Bob Burke, April 26,
2005.

5. Interview with Paul Bell,
April 5, 2005.

6. Bill Paul memoirs.

7. Ibid.

8. Text of introduction by
Valerie Couch, May 2,
2001, Heritage Archives.

9. Text of introduction by
Ralph Thompson,

October 22, 2004,
Heritage Archives.

10. Interview with Joyce
Coleson, January 18,
2006, hereafter referred
to as Joyce Coleson
interview.

11. Remarks of Bill Paul
upon induction into the
Pauls Valley Hall
of Fame, April 3, 2001,
Heritage Archives.

Chapter Twenty-One
SOME FANTASTIC
CO-WORKERS

1. Bill Paul memoirs.

2. Ibid.

3. Joyce Coleson interview.

4. Ibid.

5. Bill Paul memoirs.

Chapter Twenty-Two
FAMILY

1. Bill Paul memoirs.

2. Interview with Barbara
Paul, June 28, 2005,
hereafter referred to as
Barbara Paul interview.

3. Ibid.

4. Bill Paul memoirs.

5. Ibid.

6. Ibid.

7. Ibid.

8. Ibid.

9. Interview with Jane
Harlow, April 18, 2005.

10. Bill Paul memoirs.

11. www.casady.org, the
official Website of
Casady School.

12. Bill Paul memoirs.

13. Ibid.

14. Interview with George
Paul, July 1, 2004;
Steve Paul, July 28,
2004; Alison Paul
Miller, July 21, 2004,
and Elaine Paul Seidel,
July 19, 2004.

15. Bill Paul memoirs.

16. Ibid.

17. George Paul interview.

18. Alison Paul Miller
interview.

19. Ibid.

20. Ibid.

21. Elaine Paul Seidel
interview.

22. Ibid.

23. Ibid.

24. Ibid.

25. Steve Paul interview.

26. Ibid.

27. Ibid.

28. Bill Paul memoirs.

29. Barbara Paul interview.

INDEX